Mariusz Motyka • Hubert Michalski • Mike Koenig • Stefan Dramiński



# Panzerjäger 38(t) Hetzer & G-13

vol. I

KAGERO

**Panzerjäger 38(t) Hetzer & G-13. Vol. I • Mariusz Motyka • Hubert Michalski • Mike Koenig • Stefan Dramiński • First edition • LUBLIN 2014**

 • **ISBN 978-83-64596-13-1**

Editors: **Łukasz Gładysiak** • Translation: **Jarosław Dobrzyński** • Color profiles: **Mariusz Motyka** • Scale drawings: **Stefan Dramiński** • Design: **KAGERO STUDIO, Marcin Wachowicz**

Oficyna Wydawnicza KAGERO
**Akacjowa 100, Turka, os. Borek, 20-258 Lublin 62, Poland, phone/fax: (+48) 81 501 21 05**
www.kagero.pl • e-mail: kagero@kagero.pl, marketing@kagero.pl
**w w w . k a g e r o . p l**

Appreciating the might of tanks, which since the moments of their first appearance on the battlefield in 1916 to the end of the First World War many times rolled over the positions of emperor Wilhelm's troops on the Western Front the Germans put stress on the development of efficient methods of fighting them. Initially, using available solutions, artillery was deployed against Allied tracked vehicles. Then new weapons (antitank rifles) were designed specially to destroy armored targets and the completion of the efforts was the development of indigenous tanks, however built in symbolic numbers, unable to influence the course of the war.

After the end of the Great War and imposing limitations resulting from the Treaty of Versailles, signed in 1919 on Germany, work on antitank weapons not only had not been suspended, but evolved into development of the best possible such weapon, despite the ban. In mid 1920s under the influence of ideas of General Werner von Blomberg it was decided to design a tracked combat vehicle armed with a cannon, which thanks to high speed and mobility and low profile would be perfectly suited for eliminating tanks. This vehicle, for which a separate category named *Tankzerstörer* (tank destroyer) was created, was to have no turret and serve only defensive purposes in favorable conditions, mostly by firing from flanks.

The political and economical situation of the Weimar Republic in the latter half of 1920s did not augur the success of the project, which quickly came true. The development of the new tracked chassis turned out to be so expensive that the military budget could not afford required expenses and the Germans had to resort to half-measures, fitting guns among others to tracked bulldozer chassis. So such designs as the *3,7 cm Tak auf Hanomag WD-Schlepper 25 PS* or *7,7 cm Kanone auf Hanomag WD-Schlepper 50 PS* were developed. Tests of the vehicles built ended with a failure due to poor traction qualities of civil bulldozers and clearly showed the necessity to design a tracked chassis from scratch, even at high cost. The order to build it in late 1927 was had been issued to Krupp company, which quite quickly fulfilled this task, developing a suitable design, initially known as *Motorlafette*, later renamed *leichte Selbstfahrkanone*. However the chassis proved to be totally unsuccessful, hence after the proving ground tests it was sent back to the manufacturer in order to simplify the construction of the suspension, which was very rash. Some time later an attempt of developing a tank destroyer on the basis of the *Leichttraktor* vehicle, although after having built the prototype and conducted the tests further efforts were abandoned.

After a series of failures connected with the development of tank destroyers in early 1930s work on this kind of tracked combat vehicles had been abandoned and the situation in this field was not improved even by Adolf Hitler's rise to power in 1933. Despite commenced remilitarization, aimed among others at creation of strong armored troops (*Panzertruppen*), the dictator was not interested in the development of anti-tank weapons, since his main interest were tanks, a typically offensive weapon (till the end of the war Hitler was averse towards any defensive weapons). The situation radically changed in early 1940 in connection with the preparations to the invasion of West European countries, especially France. The German commanders expressed fears that widely used by Wehrmacht *3,7 cm Pak L/45* antitank guns probably would not be able to pierce armors of some French tanks, especially the Char B1s. Unwilling to put the success of the attack at risk and willing to prepare for the encounter with these machines, the Germans decided among others to retrofit the chassis of *Pz.Kpfw. I Ausf.B* tanks being just retired with ex-Czech 4,7 cm guns, introduced to German army's inventory after the annexation of Czechoslovakia in 1939 as *4,7 cm Pak (t)*. The official designation of thee vehicles, manufactured by Alkett factory in Berlin was *4,7 cm Pak (t) (Sfl) auf Pz.Kpfw. I (Sd.Kfz. 101) ohne Turm*, however it was quickly replaced by shorter and much catchier name *Panzerjäger I* (*Panzerjäger* – tank hunter). At the moment of the attack on France and neighboring countries Wehrmacht had four units equipped with these vehicles (*Panzerjäger-Abteilung (mot S) 521, 616, 643* and *670*). Their combat use revealed a number of shortcomings (very limited visibility, weak armor of the superstructure, pierced even by rifle bullets, cramped crew compartment), but on the other hand the combat reports showed a picture of vehicles very efficient in fighting enemy tanks, mainly thanks to outstanding guns, whose rounds were able to pierce 45 – 50 mm thick armor

**Two *Jagdpanzer 38(t) Hetzer* tank destroyers photographed in the *BMM* faktory at the end of summer 1944. Both are equipped with the early type idler wheels, the second version of mufflers and the early model *Kuggellafette IV* gun mantlet. The rear spotlights were installed on the left side of the superstructure not on the left fenders as usual. One of the vehicles has only the sand yellow (RAL 7028) overall, the second one – the three-tone camouflage scheme representing the first type applied. [Kagero Archive]**

from a distance of 500 meters (in favorable conditions even 600 meters) and had long range, enabling eliminating soft targets from a distance of up to 2 kilometers. The soldiers emphasized also high mobility and autonomousness of *Panzerjäger-Abteilung*. Willing to change position the vehicles just drove to new positions without the necessity of arduous shunting, as it was with towed guns. In case of the need of travelling a specified distance there was no need to provide towing vehicles and elaborate logistics which was the equipment without which a unit armed with towed guns could not operate.

Peculiar success of the first tank destroyer caused that high-ranking German officers began to look more favorably at this class of vehicles and gave green light for intensification of work on similar subsequent designs. In July of 1940 designing of another tank destroyer, based on the *VK 3.02* ammunition transporter chassis and a month later a vehicle of the same purpose, but based on one of variants of the *Pz.Kpfw. II* (*Pz.Kpfw. II Sonderfahrgestell 901*) began. In favor of the development of a line of tank destroyers was also the fact that after the surrender of France the German troops captured a large number of French tracked combat vehicles (and other vehicles with this traction as well), belonging mainly to the lightweight category and in most cases ready to use or requiring minor repairs. Due to the differences in technical and tactical parameters the Germans initially did not intend to introduce them to service in the *Panzertruppen*, but not taking advantage of so large number of captured tanks was not sound. In connection with it a decision was made that some would converted to tank destroyers by removal of the turret and fitting a superstructure housing a powerful antitank gun, others would be delivered to occupational forces and the chassis of remaining vehicles would serve as basis to design various special duty vehicles (e.g. self-propelled flame throwers, artillery tractors). Such thing was done with *Renault R35* tanks, which according to the order of 23 December 1940 were to be armed with proven *4,7 cm Pak (t)* gun. From February of 1941 the Alkett company was occupied with their manufacturing and by October of 1941 a total of 174 destroyers, designated *4.7 cm Pak (t) (Sfl.) auf Fgst. Pz.Kpfw. 35 R 731(f)* and 26 command vehicles (armed only with a machine gun) rolled out of the assembly hall.

By June of 1941 the development of German tank destroyers, despite creation and fielding of aforementioned types was going quite slowly. A priority for arms industry was tank production, while the *Panzerjägers* were perceived as an effective weapon, but seemed to be not necessary in the face of the military situation of that time. The greatest enemy of the Third Reich – France – had been defeated, and preparing to the attack on the USSR the Germans did not expect to encounter any combat vehicles, destruction of which would require the use of special antitank weapons. This conviction vanished after the beginning of the Barbarossa operation and encountering Soviet T-34 and KV tanks. Despite the difficulties in fighting them were vastly exaggerated during the first days of the campaign and are described in the literature in an exaggerated way until today it is undeniable that destroying these vehicles posed a serious problem for German troops. In particularly difficult situation were infantry units armed with *3,7 cm Pak L/45* guns, whose standard rounds were virtually unable to pierce KV-1 and KV-2 tank armors and could pierce the armor plates of the T-34 tanks only in favorable conditions from rather short distance.

While the Germans statistically did not encounter the tanks of the KV family in large numbers along the whole frontline, the T-34s were much more numerous and this number was steadily growing month by month. Gaining capability of destroying them forced the saturation of the army with antitank weapons. Apart from hasty introduction of new types of shells for *5 cm Pak 38* guns and repeated adaptation of the *8,8 cm Flak* anti-aircraft guns to the antitank role it was decided to significantly increase the number of the *Panzerjäger-Abteilungen* and introduce new *Panzerjägers* armed with guns capable of destroying Soviet tanks from longer distances. In December of 1941 work on a tank destroyer based on *Pz.Kpfw. II Ausf. D* chassis with Christie suspension, with captured outstanding Soviet 76.2 mm divisional gun, introduced to the inventory of the Third Reich's armed forces as *7,62 cm l.F.K* began. The first completed vehicles rolled out of *Alkett* factory in April of 1942 and after they had reached the frontline they gained a reputation of very formidable and accurate weapon. In late December of 1941 it was decided to produce a *Panzerjäger* by retrofitting the chassis of ex-Czech *Pz.Kpfw. 38 (t)* tank with this gun and in early 1942 the idea of using the chassis of captured French vehicles for construction of tank destroyers returned. This time the *Lorraine* artillery tractor was chosen; the first 15 units of the *Panzerjäger LrS für*

KAGERO

0 0,5 1 2 m

1/48 scale



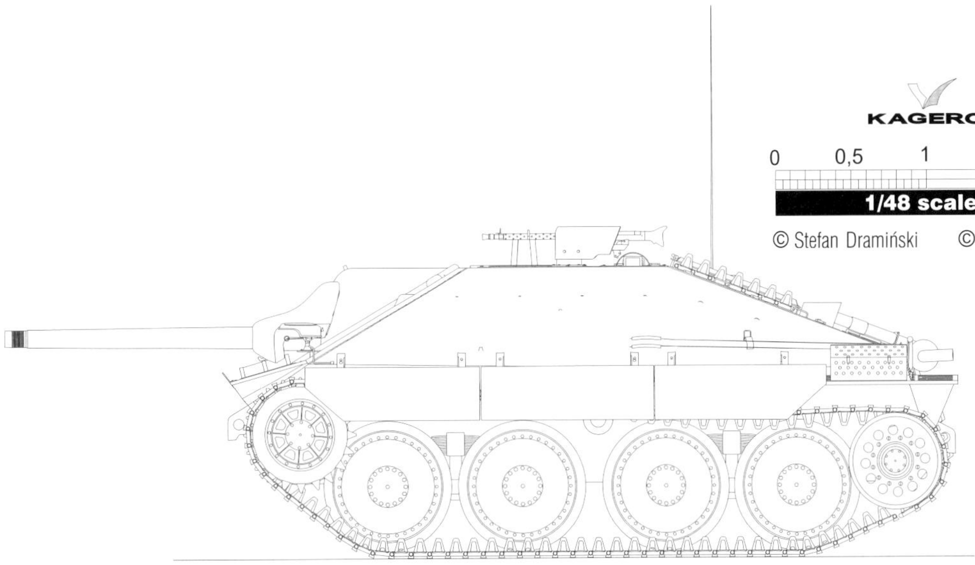

# Jagdpanzer 38 Hetzer

Traced by Stefan Dramiński

**Sheet 01**

**version 1**

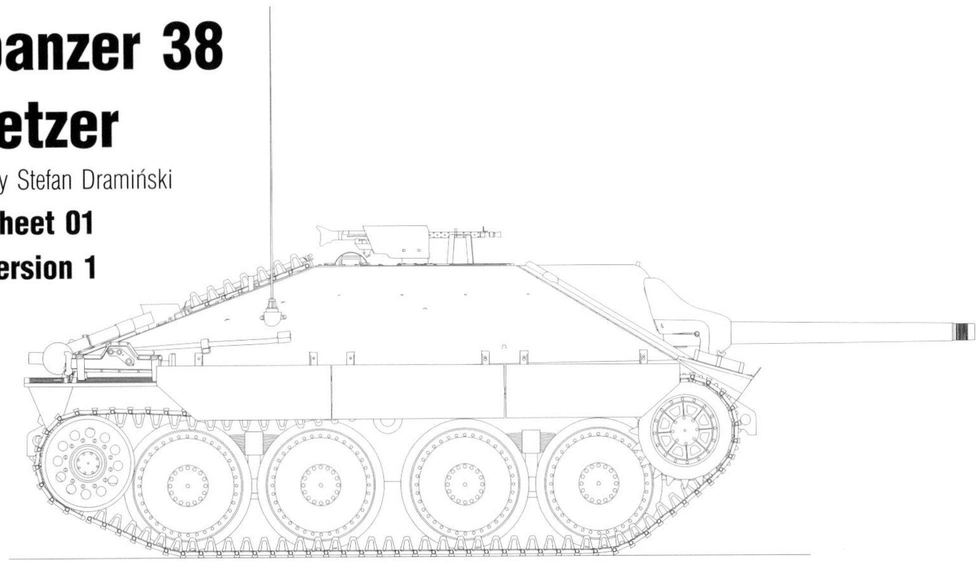

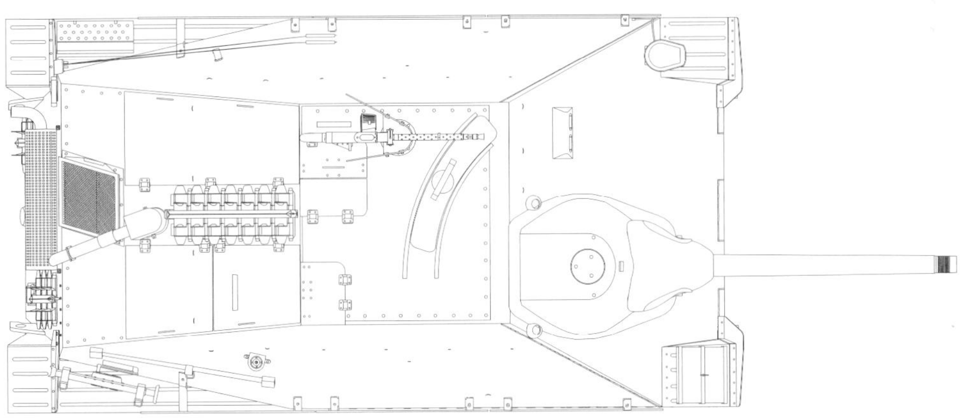

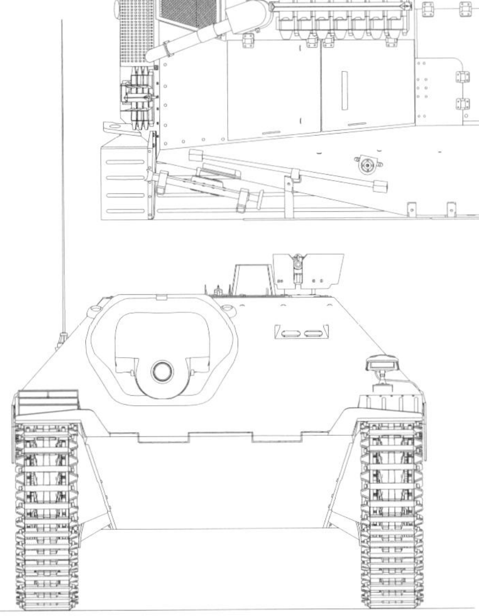

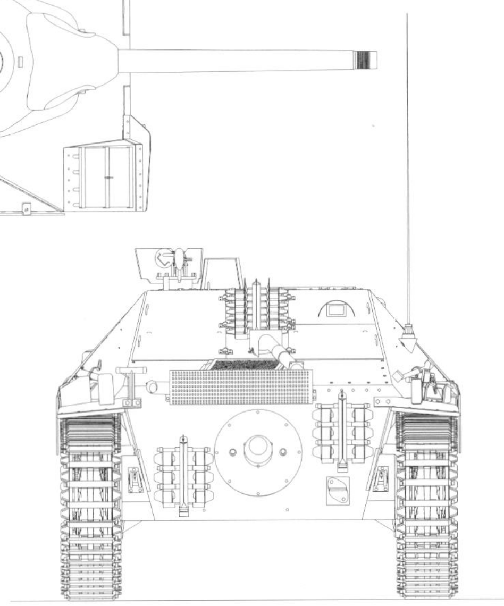

Jagdpanzer 38(t) "Hetzer". Vehicle was produced in November 1944. Production number: 321 111. [Icks collection, Patton Museum Library]

*7,5 cm Pak 40/1 (Sd.Kfz. 135)*, commonly called *Marder I* and as the designation indicated armed with outstanding *7,5 cm Pak 40/1* gun were made in June of 1942. In the same month the prototype of the *Marder II*, a tank destroyer built on the basis of *Pz.Kpfw. II* and armed with *7,5 cm Pak 40/2* gun was completed. In May of 1942 the minister of armament Albert Speer informed Hitler about the possibility of retrofitting the *Pz.Kpfw. 38(t)* chassis with *7,5 cm Pak 40* gun, so the dictator ordered to design another *Panzerjäger*. The protoplast of this vehicle, designated *Panzerjäger 38 für 7,5 cm Pak 40/3 (Sd.Kfz. 138) Ausf. H* underwent firing tests at Milovitz proving ground in late June of 1942, but production units began to roll out of assembly lines of the BMM factory only in November. In May of 1943 the *Ausf. H* version, distinguished by a superstructure situated in the middle of the hull gave way to the *Ausf. M*, easily recognizable thanks to the crew compartment shifted aft.

The aforementioned vehicles had several common basic design features. First of all each was built on the basis of a tank chassis, on which a superstructure with the main armament was fitted. The superstructure was not protected from the top with any armor plate and the crew was protected against weather conditions only by a tarpaulin sheet, which did not protect against falling shrapnel and similar hazards. The result of the fact that these vehicles were developed on the basis of light tank hulls was that they had quite weak and improperly profiled armor, providing (not always) the protection only against rifle fire. An exception was the *Nashorn* built on the chassis of *Pz.Kpfw. III/IV* which even though had all these shortcomings, was able to fight enemy vehicles from up to 2.5 km without exposing to enemy fire thanks to a mighty 8.8 cm gun. The Germans were aware that in case of introduction of new combat vehicles by the Soviets the existing *Panzerjägers* would certainly be inferior to them in most parameters decisive for the survival of a combat vehicle on the battlefield, if they would not be totally outclassed. On the other hand their previous effectiveness in combat which they owed to very good main armament did not allow resignation from development of this class of vehicles and encouraged to undertake research on their successors. Taking into consideration these and other premises from the end of 1942 German engineers began work on a new generation of tank destroyers, admittedly still based on chassis of production tanks, but of new types, like the Panther. The hull of this vehicle was roomy enough that in the tank destroyer based on it not only fitting of outstanding, long barreled 8,8cm antitank gun became possible, but also providing the crew with good protection thanks to thick and slanting armor plates, additionally enhanced by fitting of the roof. In similar convention (slanting armor plates of the hull and fitting of the roof plate) were designed most *Panzerjägers* which entered service from the end of 1943 until the end of the war, including the *Hetzer*, the further fate of which is described below.

Before reading the further text it is worth to shortly explain the matter of nomenclature of German tank destroyers and distinguishing them from self-propelled assault guns, which is very tangled. Following the chronological order the vehicles devoid of the turret and performing the role of pure antitank weapon were originally referred to as *Tankzerstörer* (tank destroyers) however this name was in force for relatively short time and ca. 1931 was replaced by the term *Selbstfahrkanone*, which literally means "self-propelled gun". With the resumption of work on this type of vehicles and the introduction of the *Panzerjäger I* the proper word describing these vehicles became *Panzerjäger*, which means "tank hunter". The development of this family of vehicles resulted in further evolution of nomenclature, so in individual vehicle designations *Pz.Slf.* or *Pak.Sfl* terms began to be used which seems to be an abbreviation of *Gepanzerter Panzerabwehrkanone auf Selbstfahrlafette* which can be translated as "armored antitank self-propelled gun". Around 1944 the word *Jagdpanzer*, which in German means the same as *Panzerjäger* entered use and was used by the Germans alternately.

According to present state of knowledge the simplest way to determine whether a given German vehicle of the Second World War period was a tank destroyer or not one should pay attention for the type of armament determining its function – if the gun it was armed with had in its designation the term *Pak*, almost for sure it was a *Panzerjäger*. In case of *K.w.K* (*Kampfwagenkanonne*) or *Stu.K.* (*Sturmgeschützkanonne*) it would be clear that we have to do with a tank or a self-propelled assault gun respectively.

## Development

It can be said that the *Jagdpanzer 38* came into being a bit accidentally and to great extent it was caused by the Allies themselves. In late November of 1943 due to a bombing raid on Berlin the *Alkett* factory manufacturing assault guns (*Sturmgeschütz*) suffered heavy damage. The damage was so severe that maintaining the previous production rate proved to be impossible which automatically resulted in reduction of deliveries of the new vehicles to the units. To return quickly to established production rate, apart from immediately commenced rebuilding of the factory, which had to take some time the Germans began to seek for a factory able to undertake the production of the assault guns and fill the production gap after the *Alkett* company. The choice fell on the *Böhmisch-Mahrische Maschinenfabrik* factory of Prague (former *CKD*), however after the familiarization with their tooling and size of assembly halls the representatives of the *OKH* decided that the production of the *Sturmgeschütz* weighing 24 tonnes was out of the question. This fact was communicated to Adolf Hitler during a meeting on 6 December 1943, who in response accepted the proposition

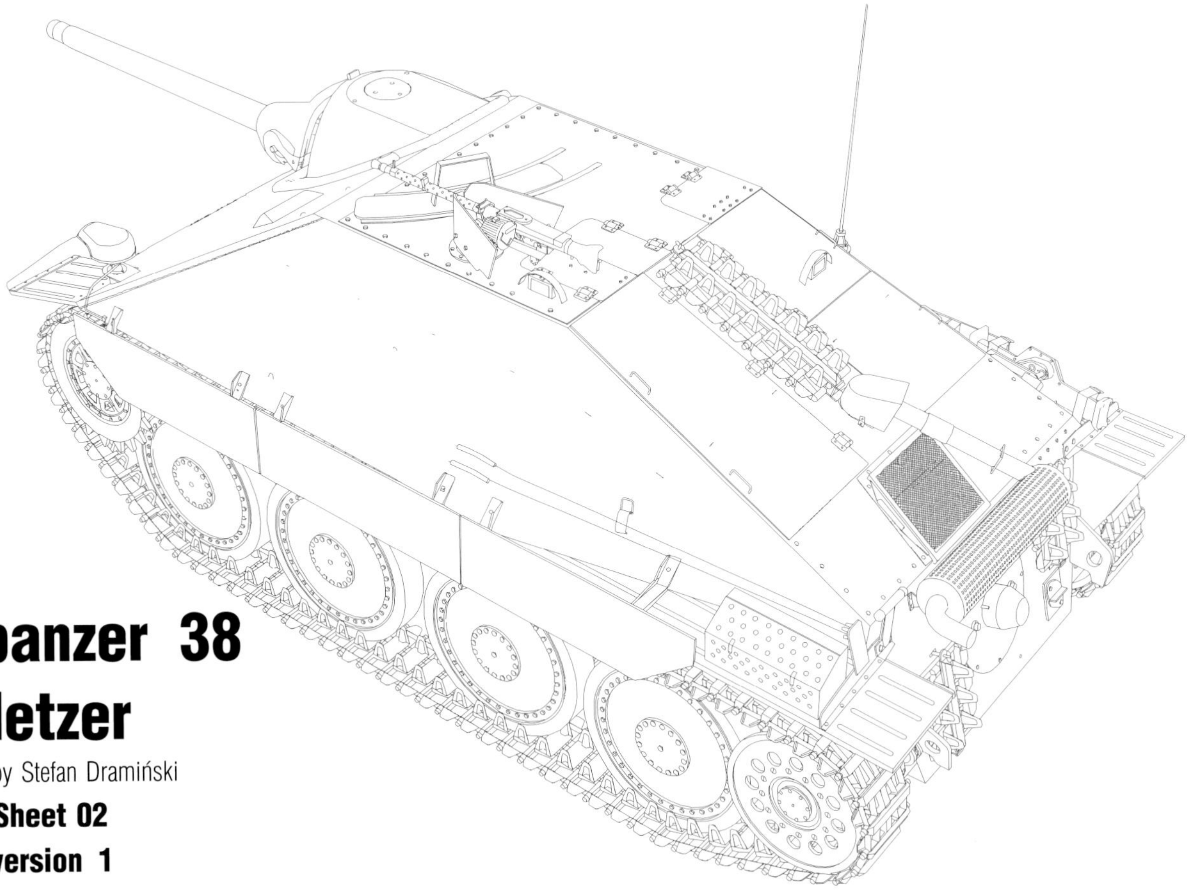

# Jagdpanzer 38 Hetzer

Traced by Stefan Dramiński

**Sheet 02**

**version 1**

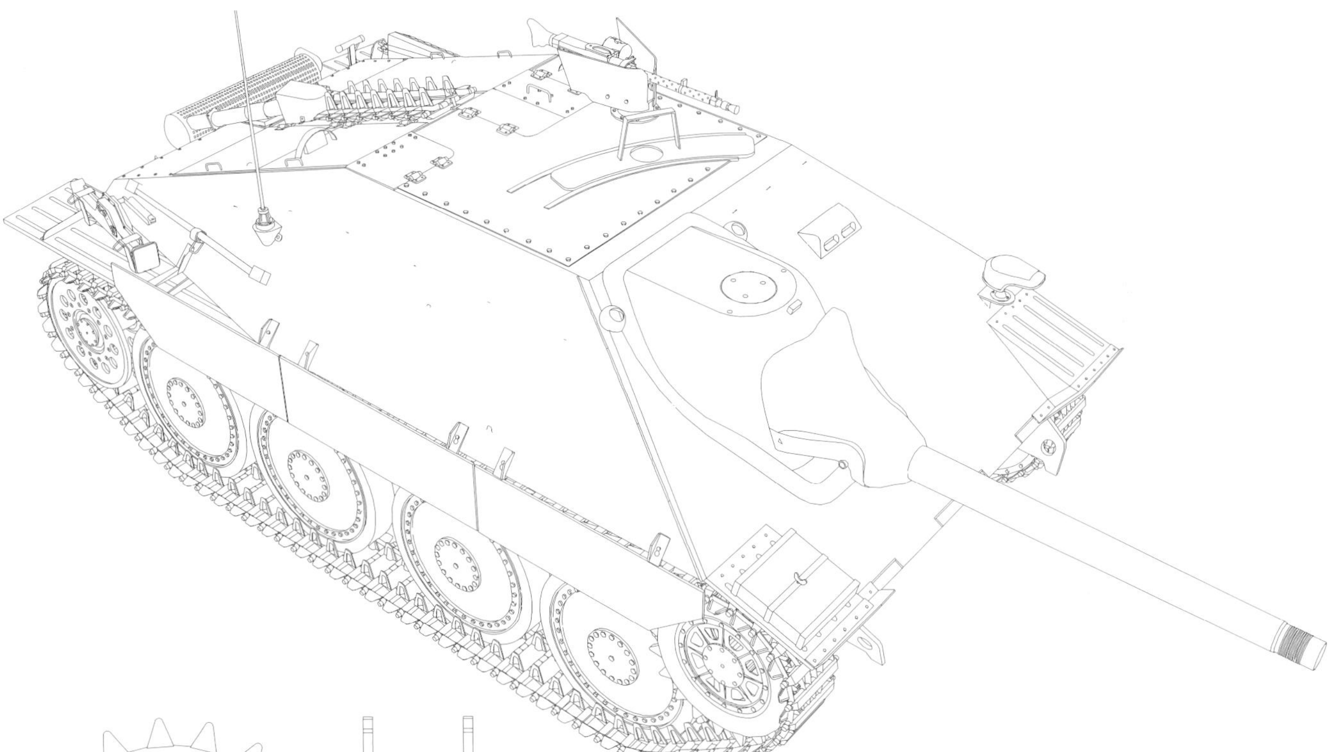

KAGERO

0 0,5 1 m

1/16 scale

*Jagpdanzer 38(t) Hetzer* **manufactured in November 1944 as the compilation of** *BMM* **supersturucture nad chasis made by** *Škoda.* **The early version of the** *Kugellafette V* **gun mantlet, the** *Rundumsfeuer* **remotely operated machine gun in front of the loader's hatch and the muffler installed in the late production series vehicles (so called** *the third type***) are clearly visible. The camouflage scheme represents the first type factory-applied in the Prague works, leaning on wide, irregular, vertical chocolate brown (RAL 8017) and dark green (RAL 6003) spots over the sand yellow (RAL 7028) base. The** *BMM* **factory, late autumn 1944. [Kagero Archive]**

of development of a new, light assault gun (*Sturmgeschütz*) weighing ca. 13 tonnes, unsophisticated enough to be manufactured by *BMM*. The technical and tactical requirements for the new vehicle were quite excessive – with the aforementioned weight it was to feature the armor consisting of slanted 60-mm thick plates and be able to attain the maximum speed of 55-60 km/h. As the main armament the *7,5 cm Pak 39* gun was planned, so the qualification of the vehicle was changed from the self-propelled assault gun to tank destroyer (as it was already mentioned each vehicle armed with a *Pak* gun was a tank destroyer; if the *Stu.K* gun was used, it would remain an assault gun). It is worth mentioning that at that time (late 1943) the differences in the roles of a tank destroyer and assault gun virtually did not exist – both categories of vehicles due to dramatic frontline situation performed virtually the same tasks.

The first technical drawings of the vehicle were showed Adolf Hitler on 17 December 1943. So quick pace of the design work was possible thanks to the use of elements of relatively simple chassis of the *Pz.Kpfw. 38(t) alter Art* and *Pz.Kpfw. 38(t) neuer Art*. The former was a standard *Pz.Kpfw. 38(t)*, widely used by the *Panzertruppen* during 1939-1942 and the latter was its modernized development version intended for armed reconnaissance. The vehicle was initially designated *Stürmgeschutz 38*, which was later changed to *Jagdpanzer 38*, but for a while both designations were used alternately. After the introduction the vehicle was named *Hetzer* by the soldiers.

The project was accepted by the dictator and directed to further development. In the third decade of January the construction of a wooden mockup was completed which even before the end of the month (on 26 January 1944) was showed the representatives of the Army Ordnance Department (*Heeres Waffenamt*). It was decided then to order three prototypes which were to commence trials in March. The order was fulfilled properly and in April of 1944 the completed vehicles were accepted by members of the aforementioned institution.

From the moment of the beginning of the program of the development of the destroyer Adolf Hitler insisted on possibly quickest launch of the production even for the price of shortening or even incompletion of the proving ground tests. On 18 January 1944 a decision about placing an order for 1,000 vehicles at the BMM factory was made and ten days later the Führer deemed the commencement and gradual increase of the vehicle's production the leading task for the army. The original contract was soon increased by further 1,000 units; in total the BMM factory was to build 2,000 vehicles with chassis numbers (*Fgst. Nr.*) from 321001 to 323000. Interesting is that within this order it was planned to build not only the tank destroyers but also technical support vehicles (*Bergepanzerwagen 38*) and *Jagdpanzers 38 starr* (described hereinafter), which were actually ordinary Hetzers with modified armament.

In the spring or early summer of 1944 *Škoda* also was granted a contract for 2,000 destroyers with chassis numbers from 323001 to 325000. Approximately at the same time the representatives of the BMM and army signed a contract for the delivery of further 2,000 *Hetzers* with serial numbers from 325001 do 327000. W July of 1944 *Škoda* received an order for further 2,000 vehicles (*Fgst. Nr.* 327001 – 329000). The last order for *Hetzers* was placed in October of 1944 and amounted to 3,000 units. They probably were to receive chassis numbers from 329001 to 33200. After summing up all contracts we receive a number of 11,000 *Jagdpanzers 38* ordered.

The true volume of the production differed much from envisaged. As it was already mentioned the first three *Hetzers* were built at the BMM factory in March of 1944. A month later, in April, 20 vehicles were completed. In May, June, July, August, September, October, November and December of 1944 respectively 20, 100, 100, 150, 190, 133, 298 and 223 were completed. In 1945 during the months of January, February and March respectively 289, 273 and 148 vehicles were completed. Due to a bombing raid on the BMM factory in April the exact number of vehicles built during that and the next month is not known, but it is estimated that in April and May of 1945 at least 70 vehicles were built. Summing up, from March of 1944 to May of 1945 no less than 2,047 *Hetzers* were completed at this factory.

At the *Škoda* factory the production of the *Jagdpanzer 38s* began in July of 1944 with completion of 10 units. In August,

KAGERO

0 0,5 1 2 m

1/48 scale



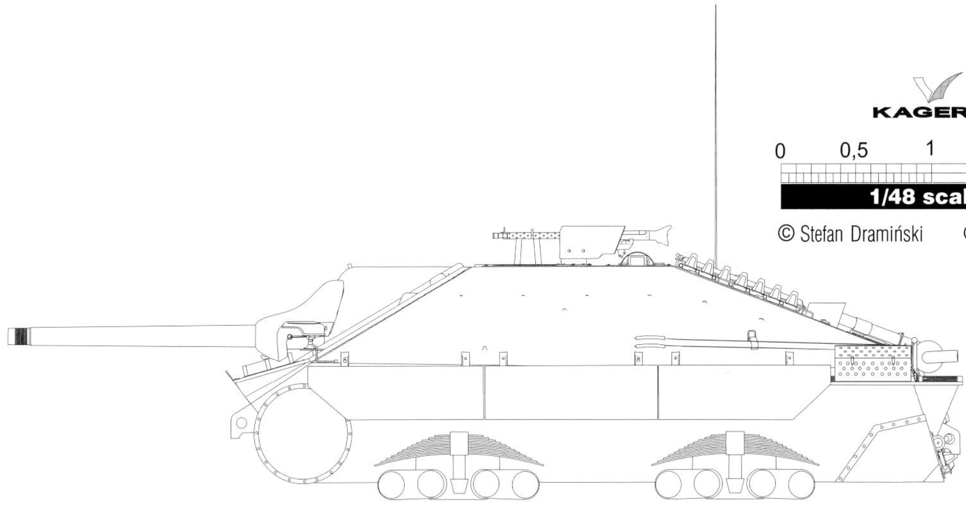

# Jagdpanzer 38 Hetzer

Traced by Stefan Dramiński

**Sheet 03**

**version 1**

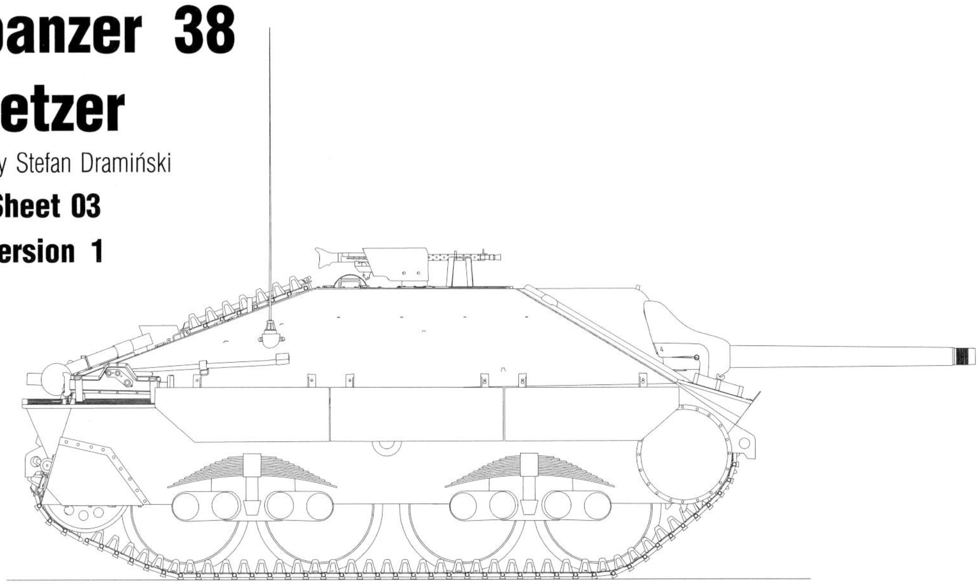

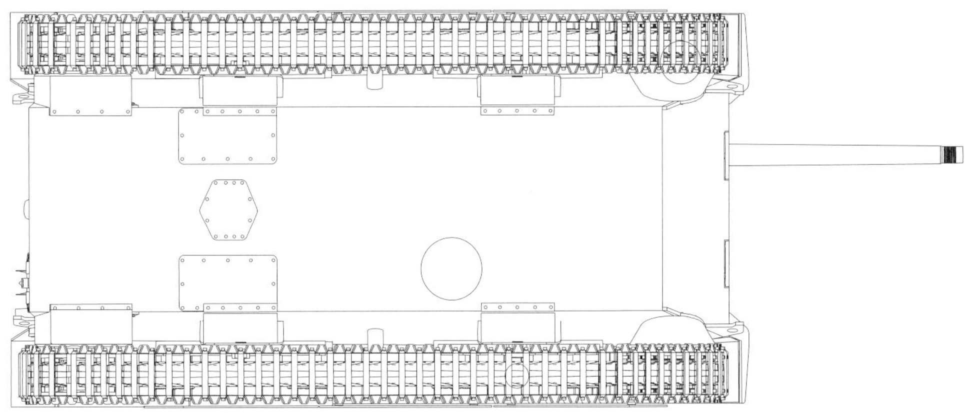

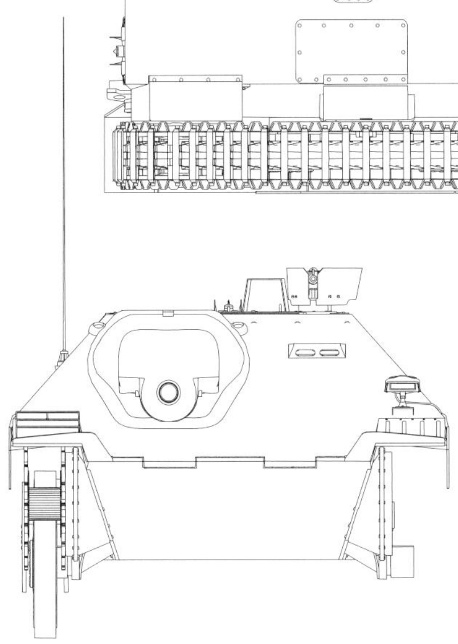

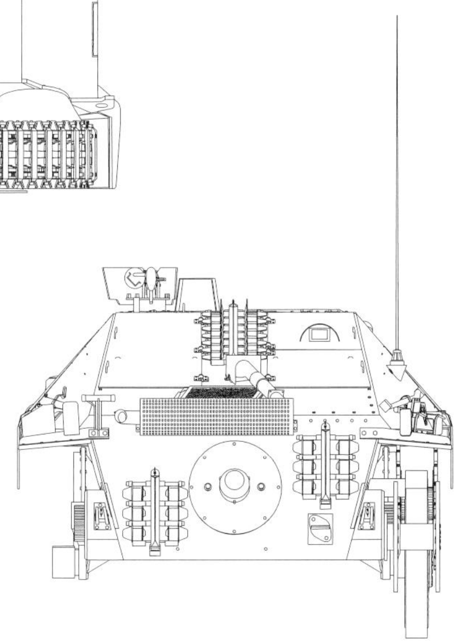

Jagdpanzer 38 "Hetzer", early production version. Vehicle captured by American army. [Icks collection, Patton Museum Library]

September, October, November and December of 1944 the company built respectively 20, 30, 57, 89 and 104 destroyers. In January, February and March of 1945 respectively 145, 125 and 153 vehicles were completed. Since *Škoda,* like BMM fell victim of an Allied bombing raid in April the exact number of vehicles built during these two months is not known, but it is known that at least 47 vehicles were completed. Summing up, from July of 1944 to May 0f 1945 this company completed at least 780 *Hetzers.*

## Technical description

**General characteristics**: The *Jagdpanzer 38* tank destroyer had following tactical and technical parameters: the vehicle's weight amounted to 16 tonnes (three tonnes more than envisaged), dimensions (length with the gun barrel, width and height respectively) were 6.27 m, 2.63 m and 2.10 m. The vehicle was capable of rolling over ditches up to 1.3 m wide and overcoming vertical obstacles up to 65 cm wide and water obstacles up to 90 cm deep. The ground clearance was 0.38 m. The crew comprised four men: the commander, gunner, loader and driver. Embarking and disembarking was through two two-piece hatches on top.

**Armament**: the main armament of the *Hetzer* was *7,5 cm Pak 39* gun with barrel length of 48 calibers, mounted on the front of the vehicle. Its weight was 1,235 kg, maximum range 6,600 m and the rate of fire – 10 to 15 rounds per minute. The barrel's life was estimated at about 5,000 – 7,000 rounds fired. The range of movement in the horizontal plane was $5^0$ left and $11^0$ right and the vertical plane from – $6^0$ to $+12^0$. The target was localized by the commander with *Sf. 14 Z* periscopic optical gun sight and was acquired by the gunner with *Sfl. Z.F.1a.* periscopic sight. Following types of rounds were used:

- armor piercing *7,5 cm Pzgr.39* (weight – 6.80 kg, muzzle velocity – 750 m/s),
- sub-caliber armor piercing *7,5 cm Pzgr.40* (weight – 4.10 kg, muzzle velocity – 930 m/s),
- shaped charge armor piercing *7,5 cm Gr.38 HL/B* (weight – 4.57 kg, muzzle velocity – 450 m/s),
- shaped charge armor piercing *7,5 cm Gr.38 HL/C* (weight – 5.00 kg, muzzle velocity – 450 m/s),
- high explosive fragmentation *7,5 cm Spr. Gr.39* (muzzle velocity – 450 m/s),

The ammunition reserve for the gun amounted to 41 rounds. As the secondary armament 7.92 mm *MG-34* (or *MG-42*) machine gun with 600 rounds was mounted on the top on the right side. The machine gun was operated from inside. In the vehicle also individual weapons in the form of 9-mm MP-40 submachine guns with 192 rounds (six magazines), which at the end of the war were often replaces by MP-44 assault rifles.

**The suspension** comprised eight road wheels mounted in pairs on four bogies, cushioned by leaf springs, two drive sprockets mounted in the front and two idler wheels mounted in the rear. The whole drive assembly was encircled by two belts of small – link, single – bolt, single – fence *Kgs 350/140* tracks with 96 links in each. Due to the heavy gun with its yoke, most transmission elements and relatively thick armor plates mounted in the front the front bogies and wheels were overloaded. The ground pressure amounted to 0.76 kg/cm$^2$.

**Powerplant and transmission:** one rear mounted, liquid – cooled six – cylinder *Praga AC 2800* petrol engine with displacement of 7754 cm$^3$, rated at 160 hp at 3,000 RPM. The bore was 110 millimeters and the stroke was 136 millimeters. The engine was supplied with fuel from two tanks of total capacity of 320 liters. The power was delivered by the drive shaft running through the crew compartment from the engine to front - mounted five-gear (plus one reverse gear) Praga-Wilson gearbox and then to the steering mechanism and lateral transmissions, which delivered power to drive sprockets. The fuel consumption amounted to ca. 1.77 l/km (on road) or 2.46 l/km (in terrain) and the power/weight ratio amounted to 9,4 km/tonne. The vehicle attained the speed of 40 km/h and average speed of 20-30 km/h on road. In terrain the average speed was 15 km/h and the range, depending on the surface was below 180 km (on road) and 130 km (in terrain).

The armor consisted of rolled plates of following thickness and iclination: the front armor plate - 60 mm/$60^0$, front lower armor plate – 60 mm/$40^0$, side slanted armor plates – 20 mm/$40^0$, side vertical armor plates – 15 mm/$0^0$, rear lower plate protecting the powerplant: 15 mm, rear upper plate protecting the powerplant: 8 mm/$70^0$, bottom – 10 mm, top – 8 mm.

Detailed description of Jagdpanzer 38(t) Hetzer as well as its combat use will be presented in the second volume of this book.

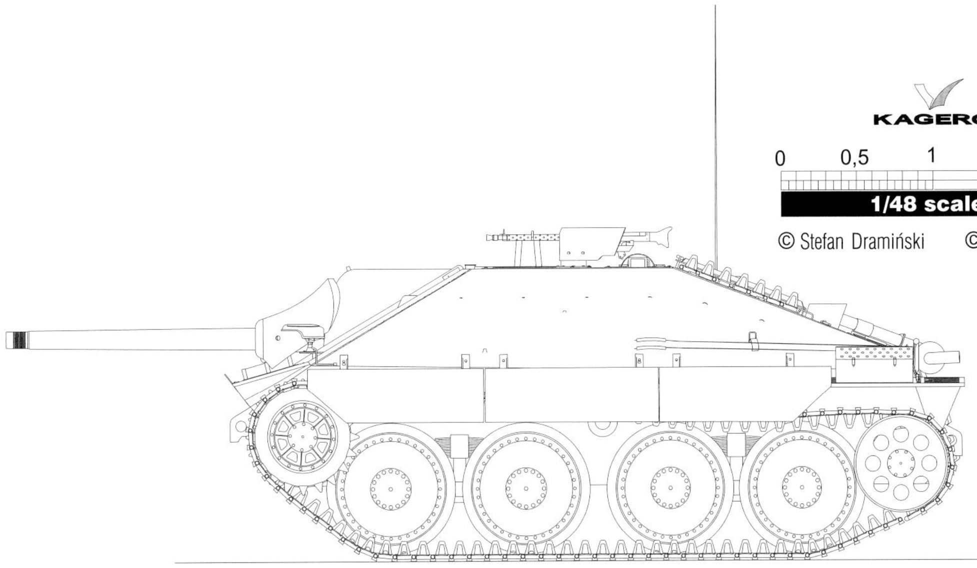

KAGERO

0 0,5 1 2 m

1/48 scale



# Jagdpanzer 38 Hetzer

Traced by Stefan Dramiński

**Sheet 04**

**version 2**

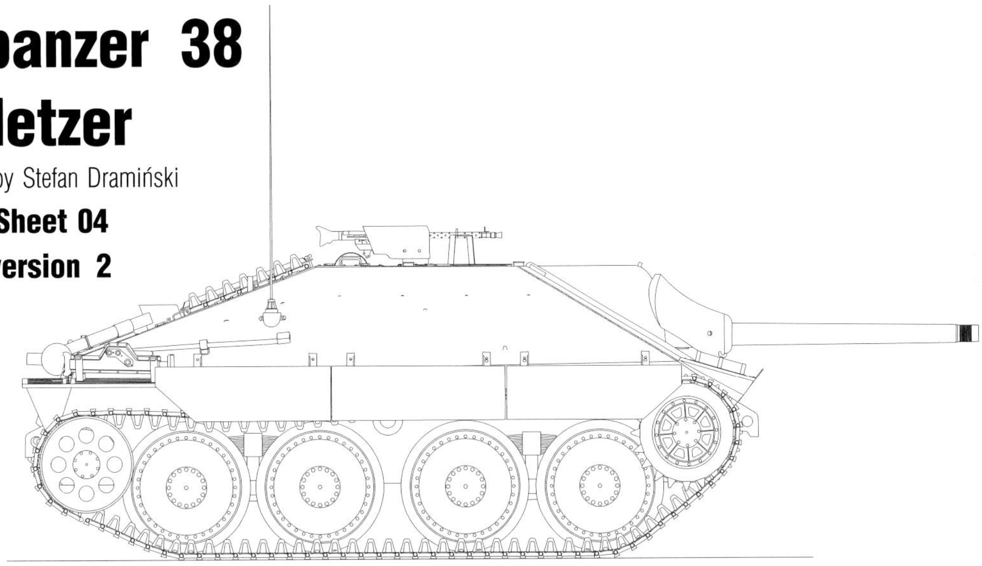

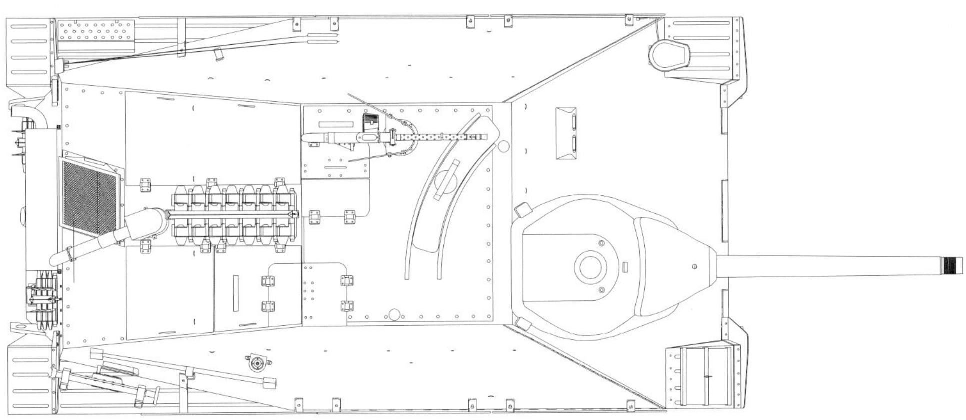

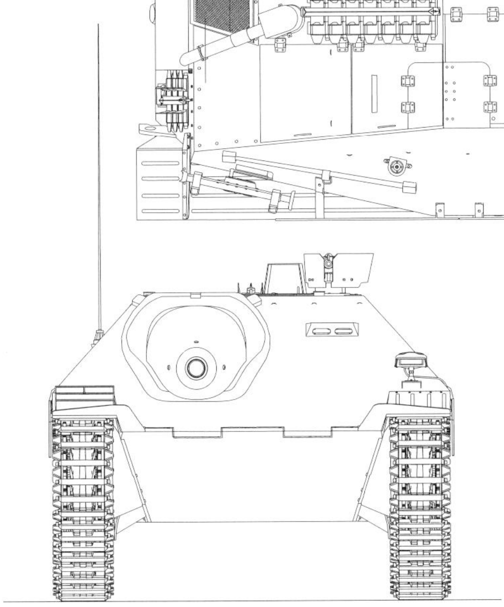

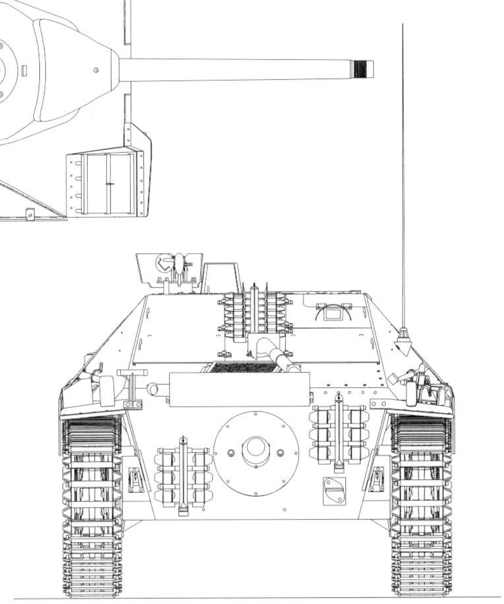

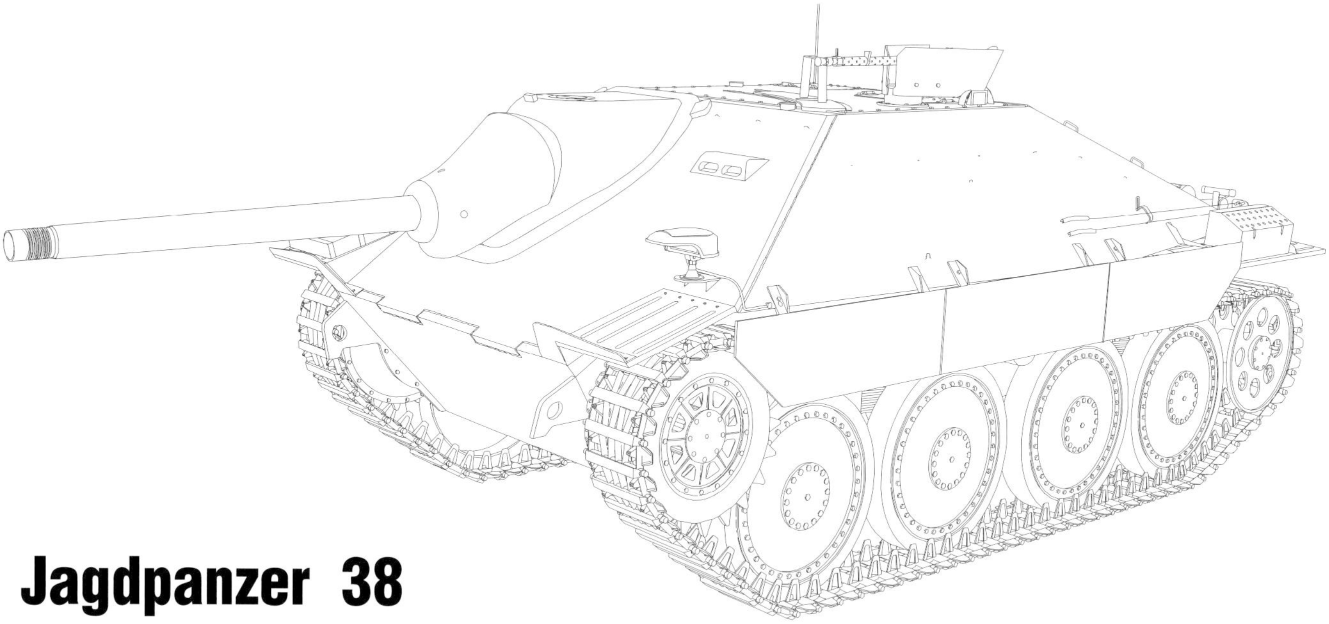

# Jagdpanzer 38 Hetzer

Traced by Stefan Dramiński

**Sheet 05**

**version 2**

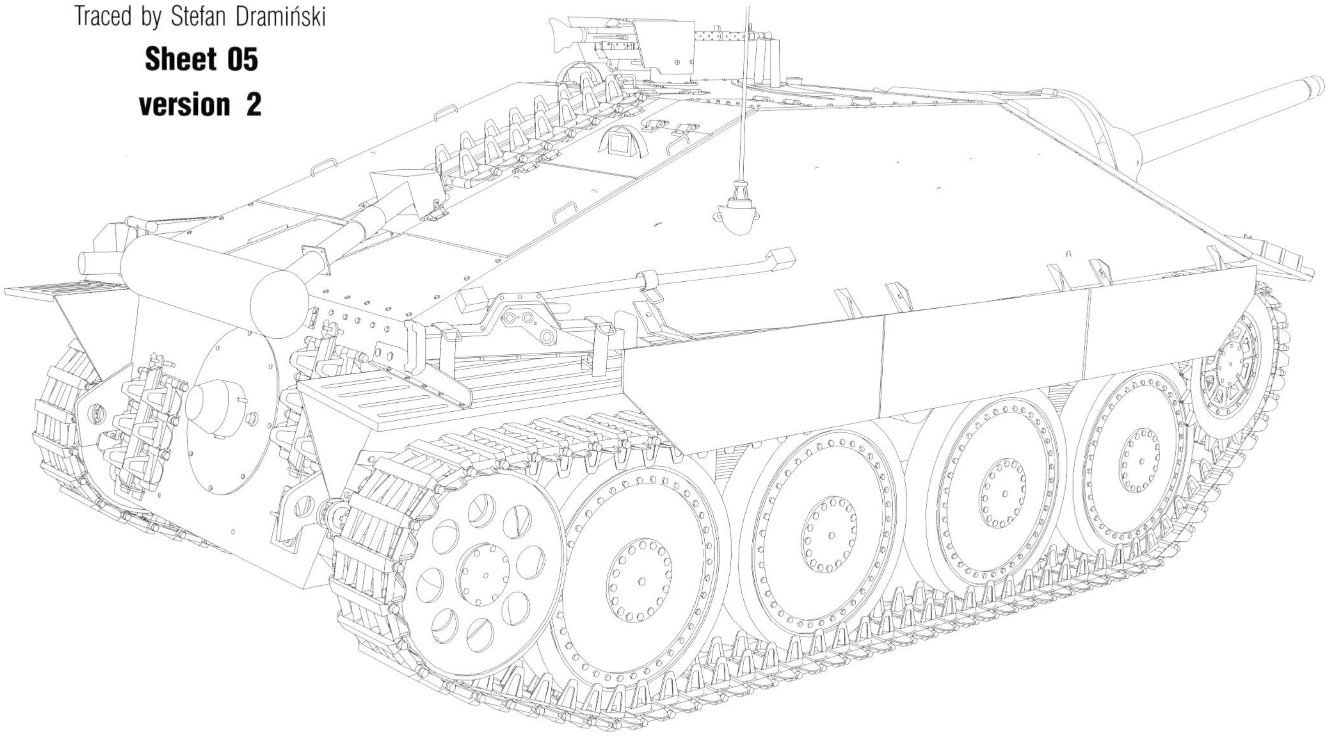

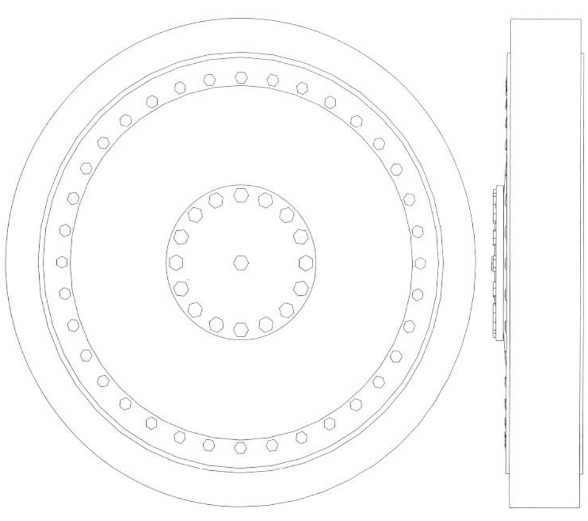

KAGERO

0 0,5 1 m

**1/16 scale**

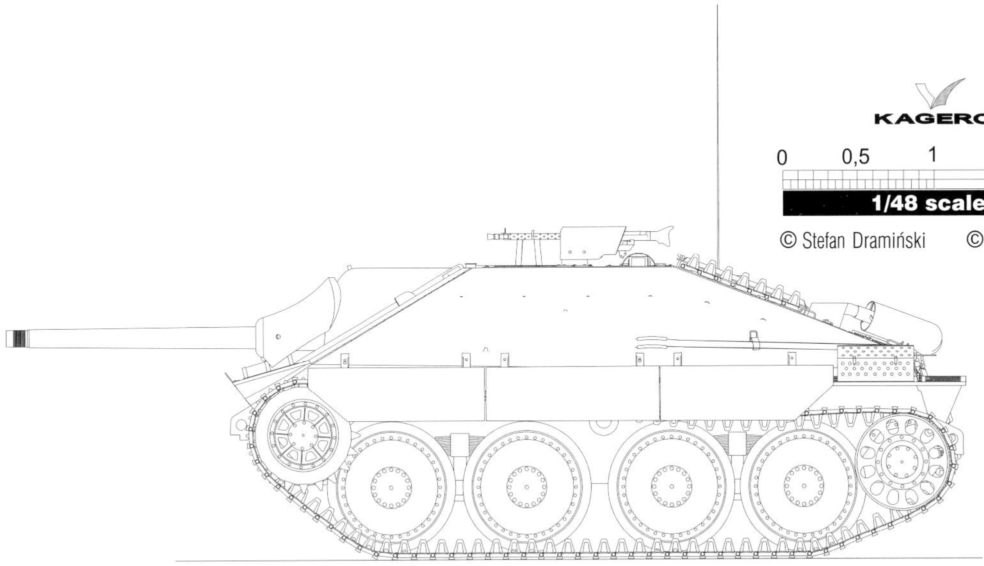

0 0,5 1 2 m

1/48 scale



# Jagdpanzer 38 Hetzer

Traced by Stefan Dramiński

**Sheet 06**

**version 3 – early**

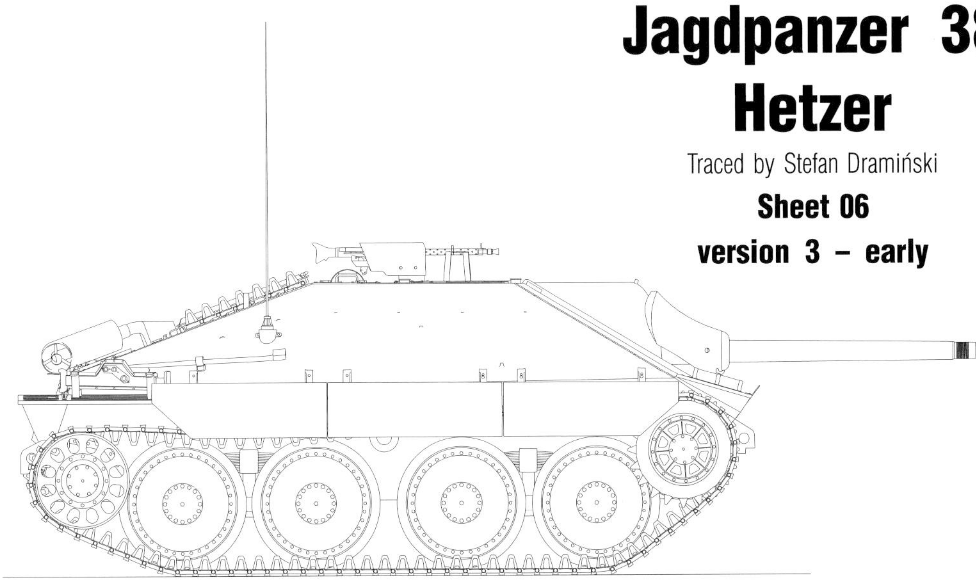

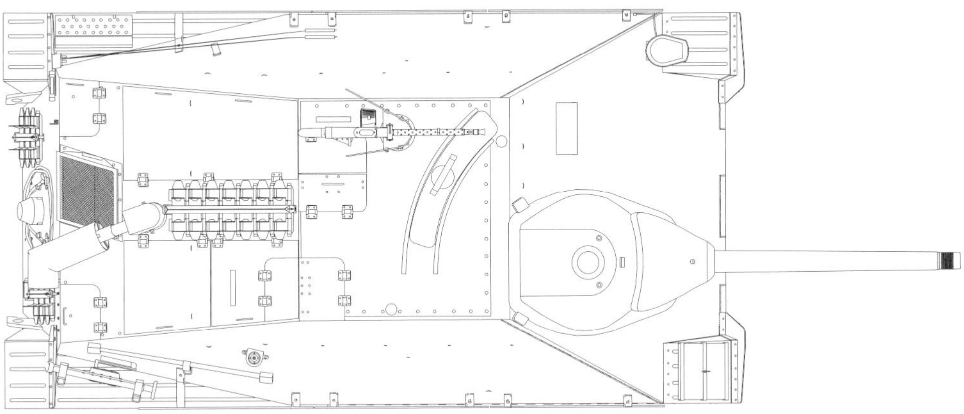

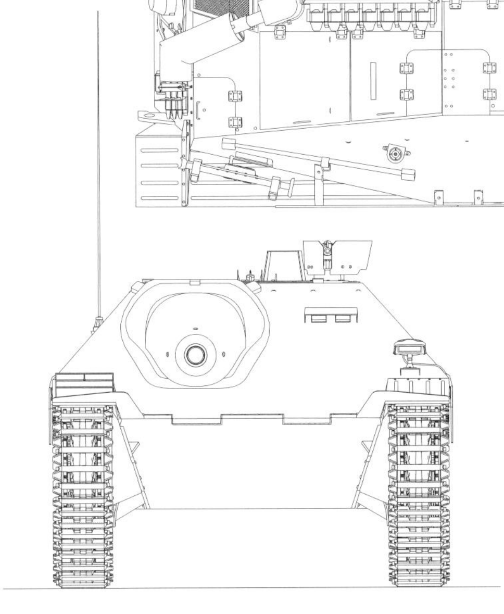

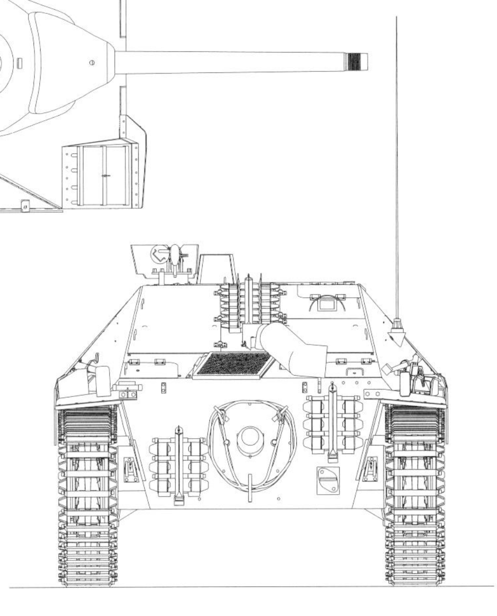

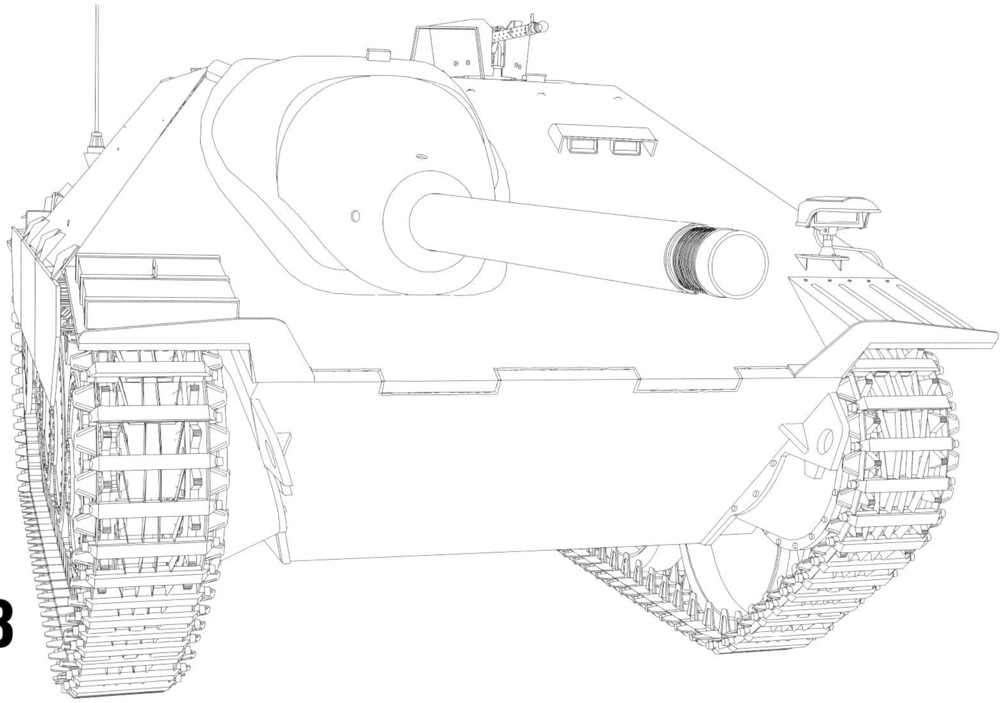

# Jagdpanzer 38 Hetzer

Traced by Stefan Dramiński

**Sheet 07**

**version 3 - early**

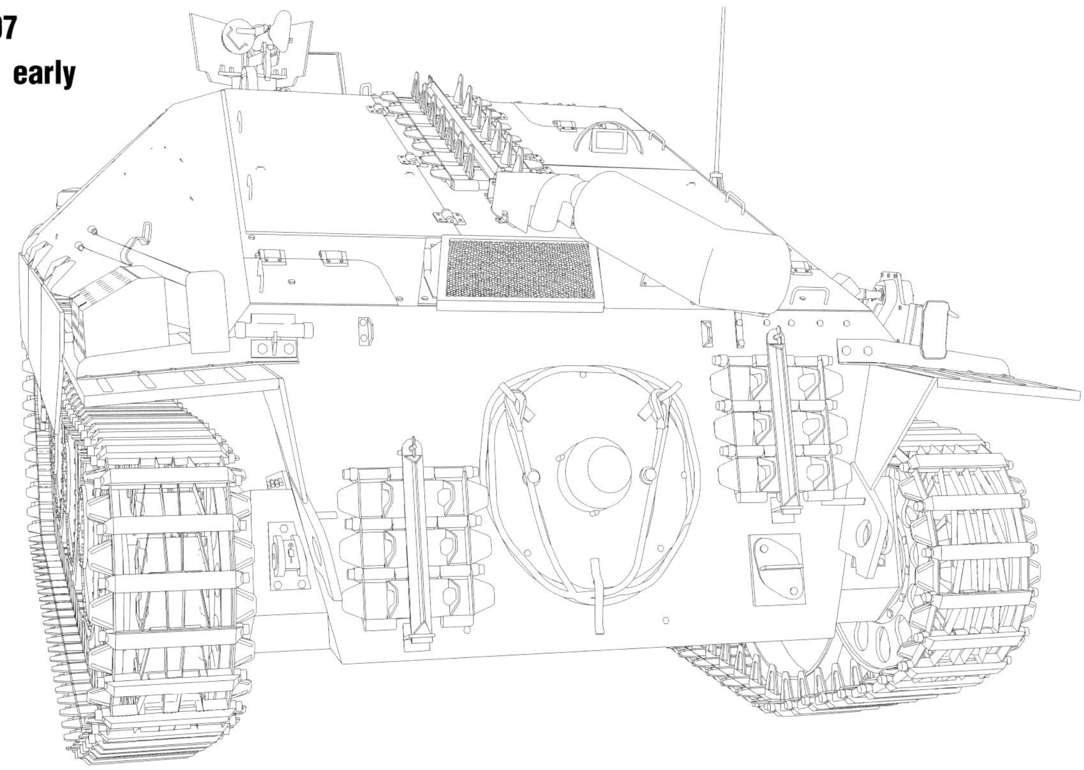

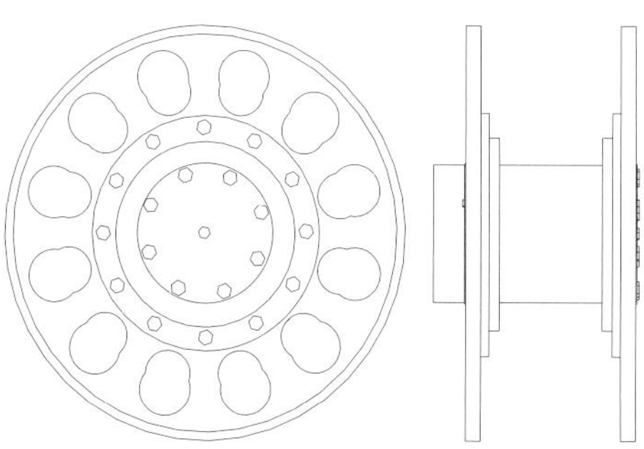

0 0,5 1 m

**1/16 scale**

0 0,5 1 2 m

1/48 scale



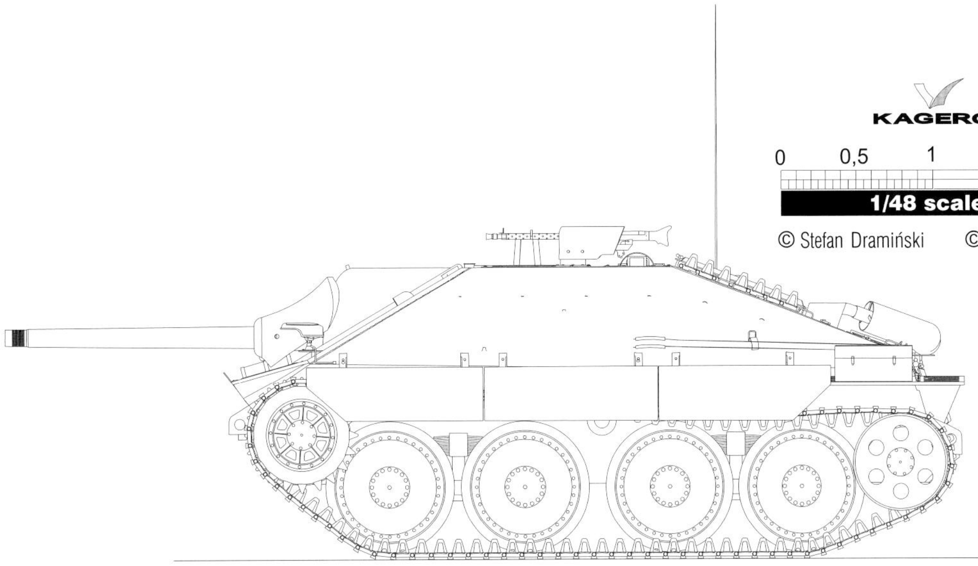

# Jagdpanzer 38 Hetzer

Traced by Stefan Dramiński

**Sheet 08**

**Version 3 – late**

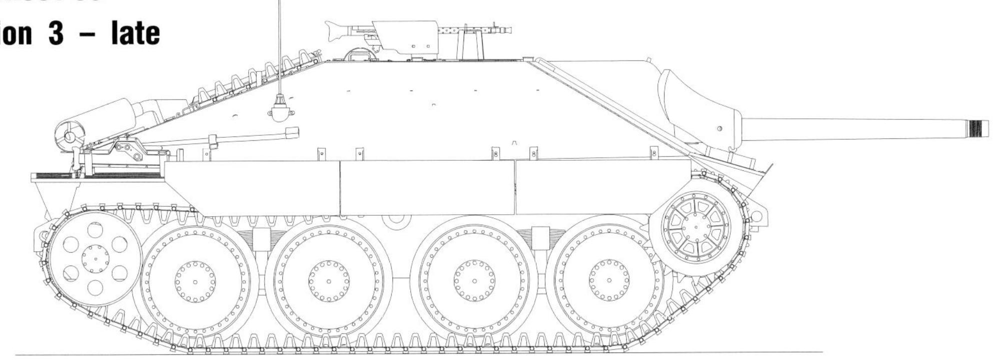

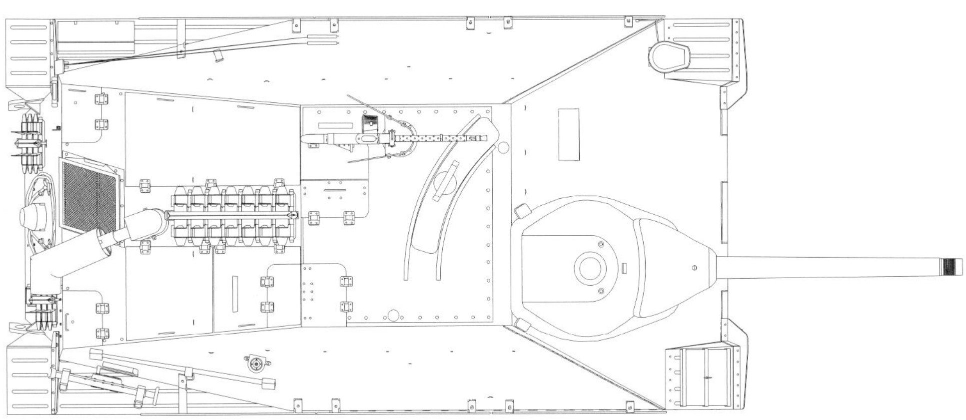

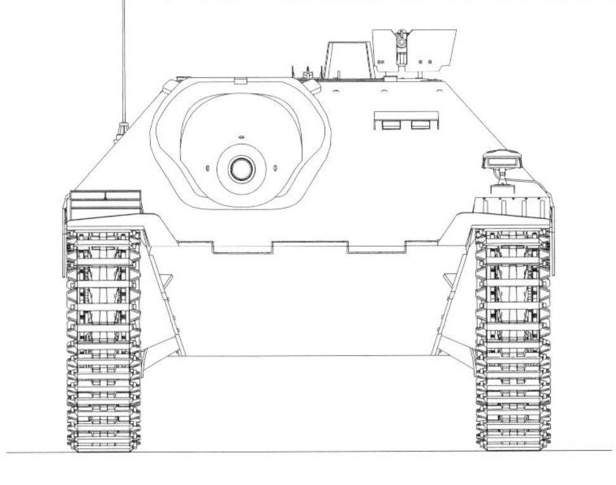

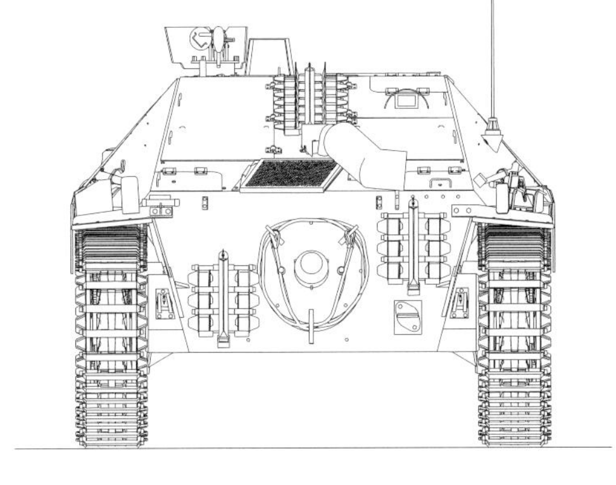

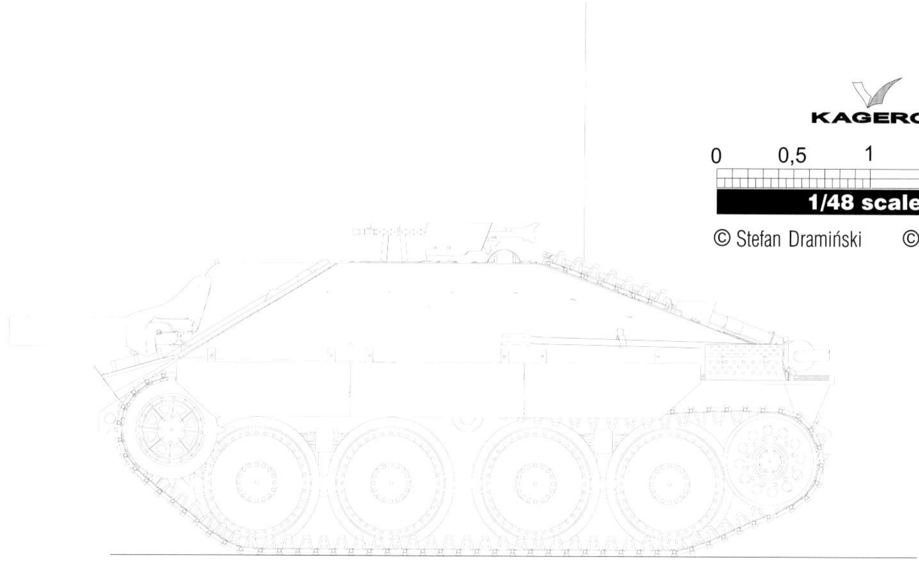

KAGERO

0 0,5 1 2 m

1/48 scale



# StuH 42/2 auf Jagdpanzer 38

Traced by Stefan Dramiński

**Sheet 09**

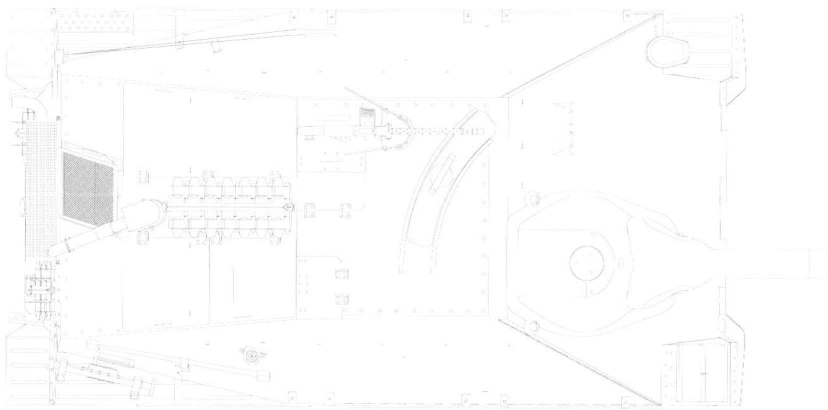

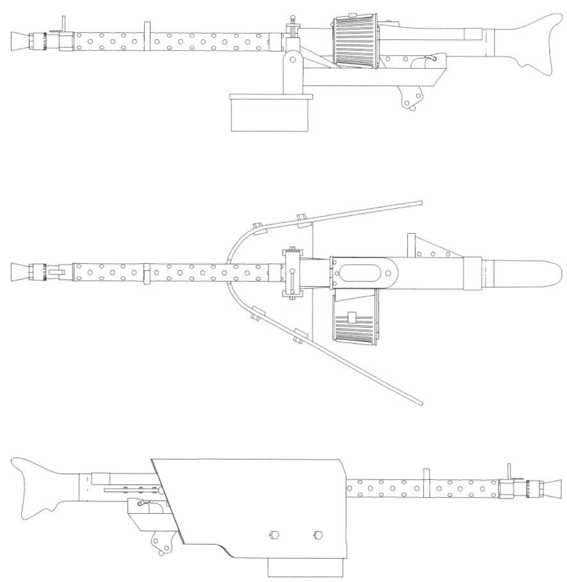

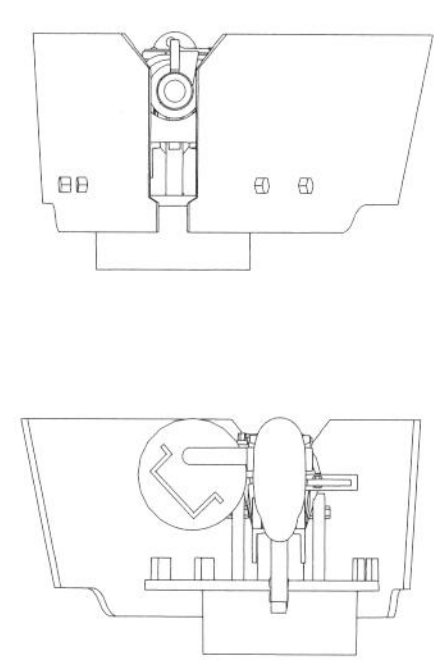

KAGERO

0 0,5 1 m

1/16 scale

0 0,5 1 2 m

**1/48 scale**



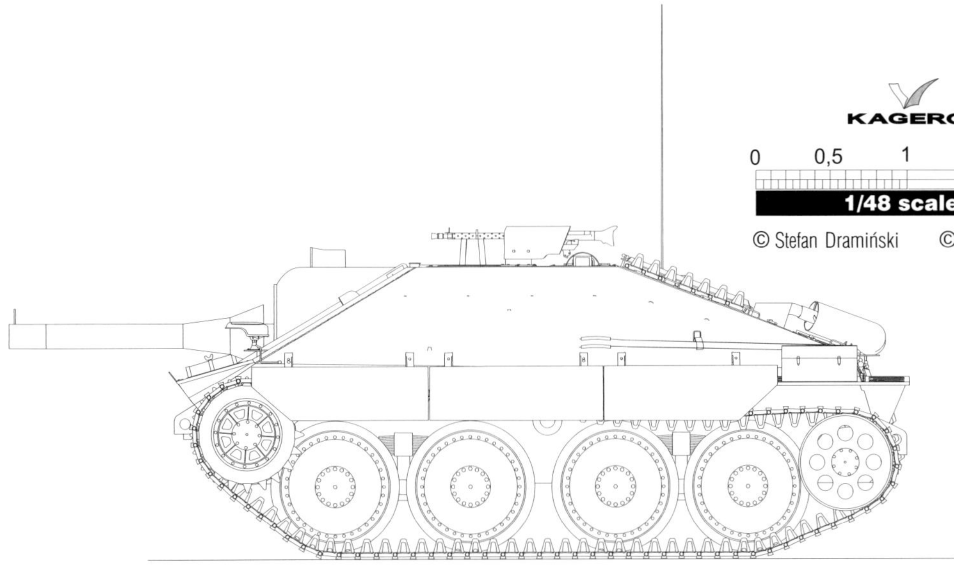

# Flammpanzer 38

Traced by Stefan Dramiński

**Sheet 10**

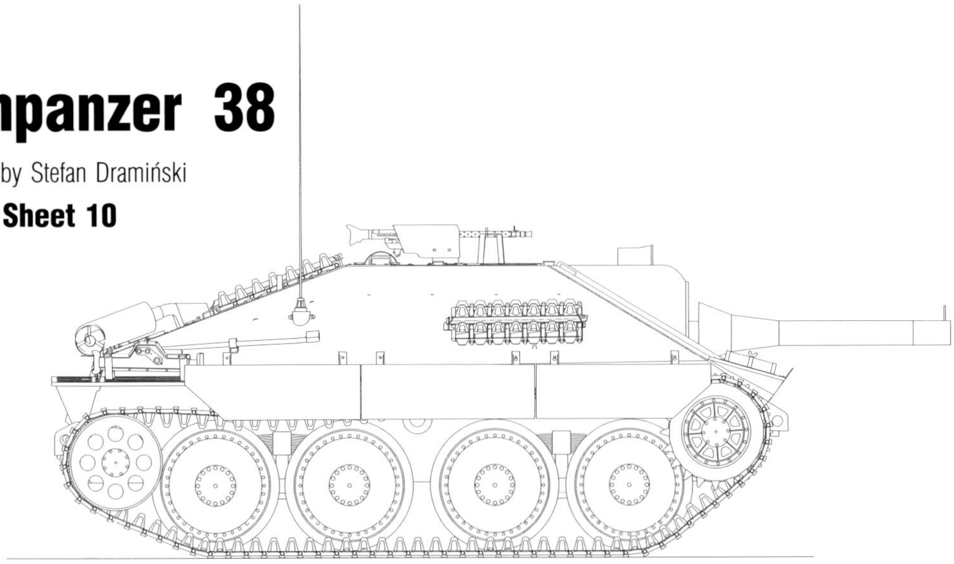

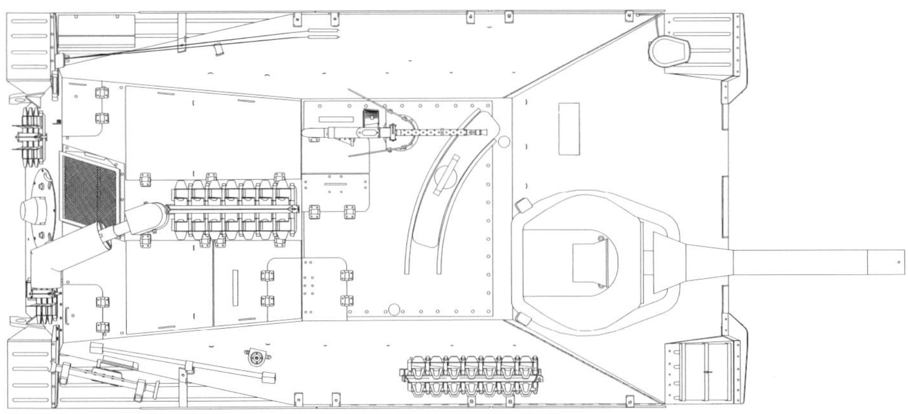

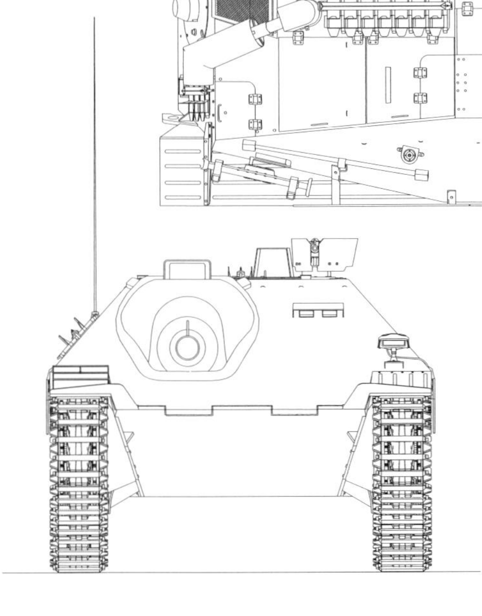

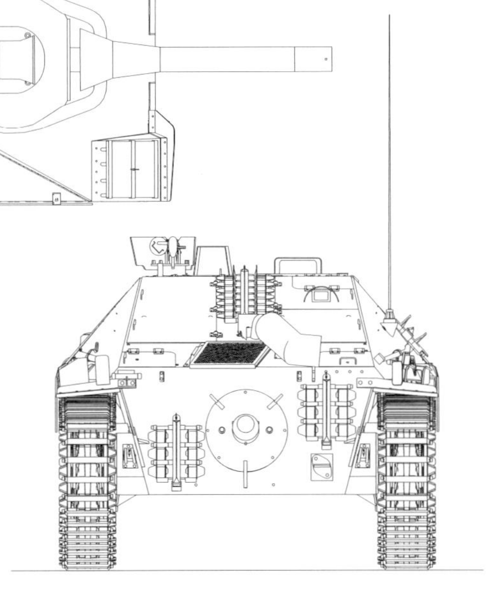

KAGERO

0 0,5 1 2 m

1/48 scale



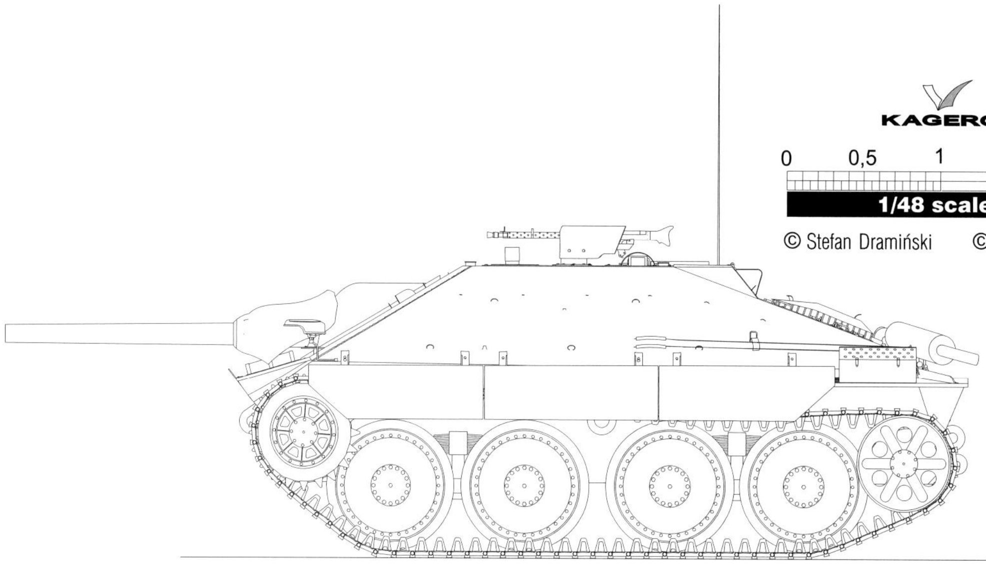

# Jagdpanzer 38 Starr

Traced by Stefan Dramiński

**Sheet 11**

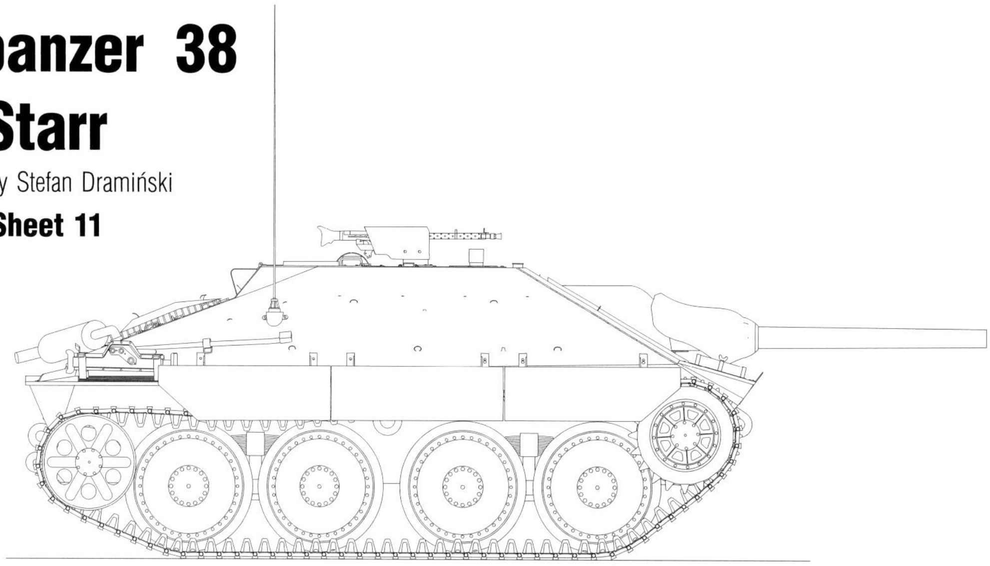

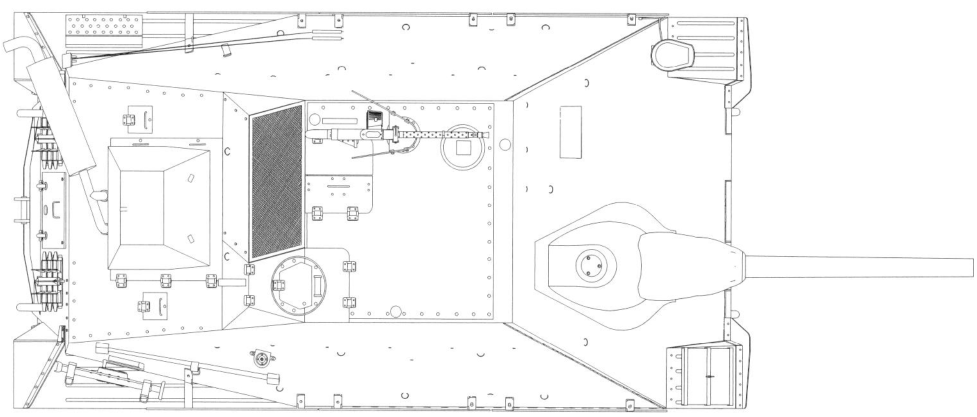

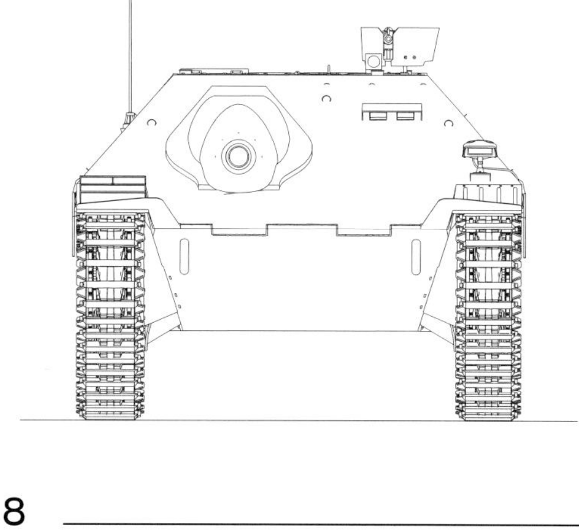

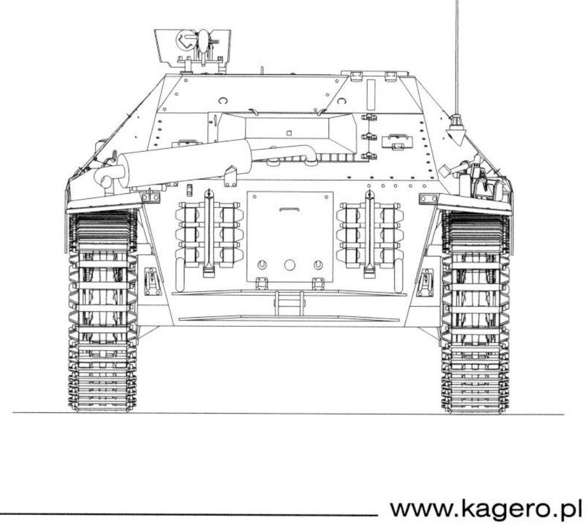

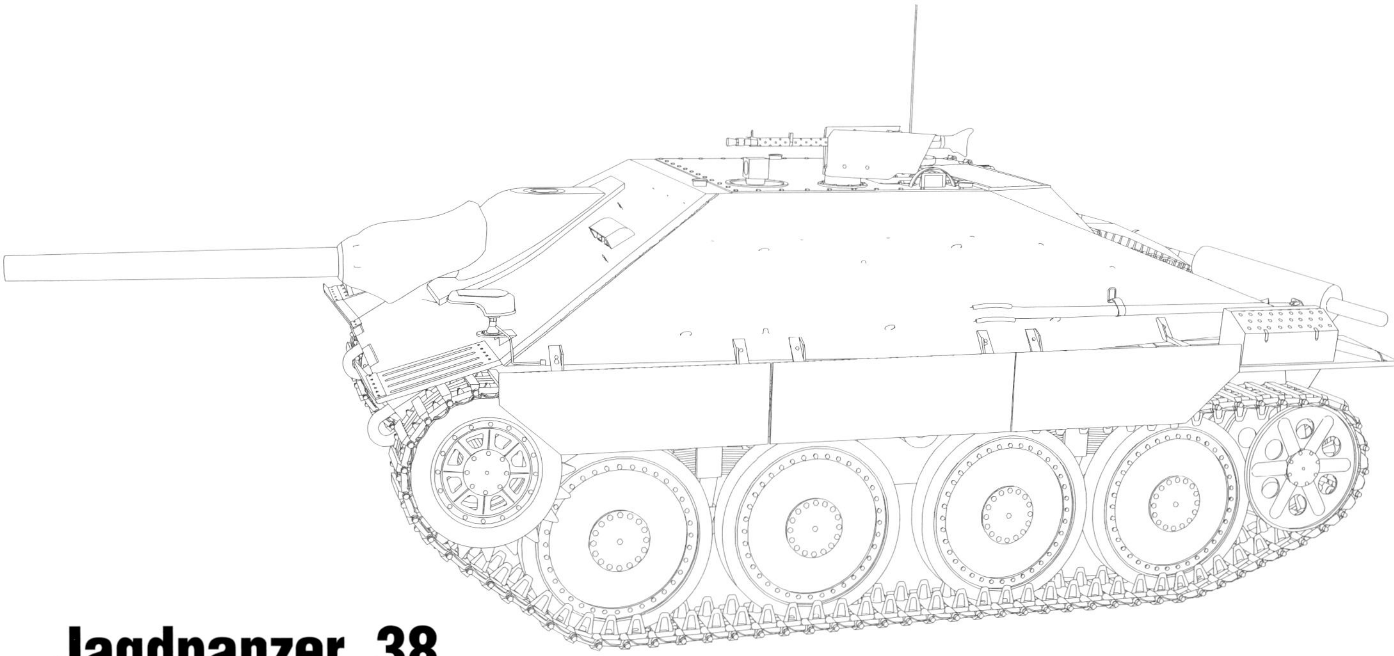

# Jagdpanzer 38 Starr

Traced by Stefan Dramiński

**Sheet 12**

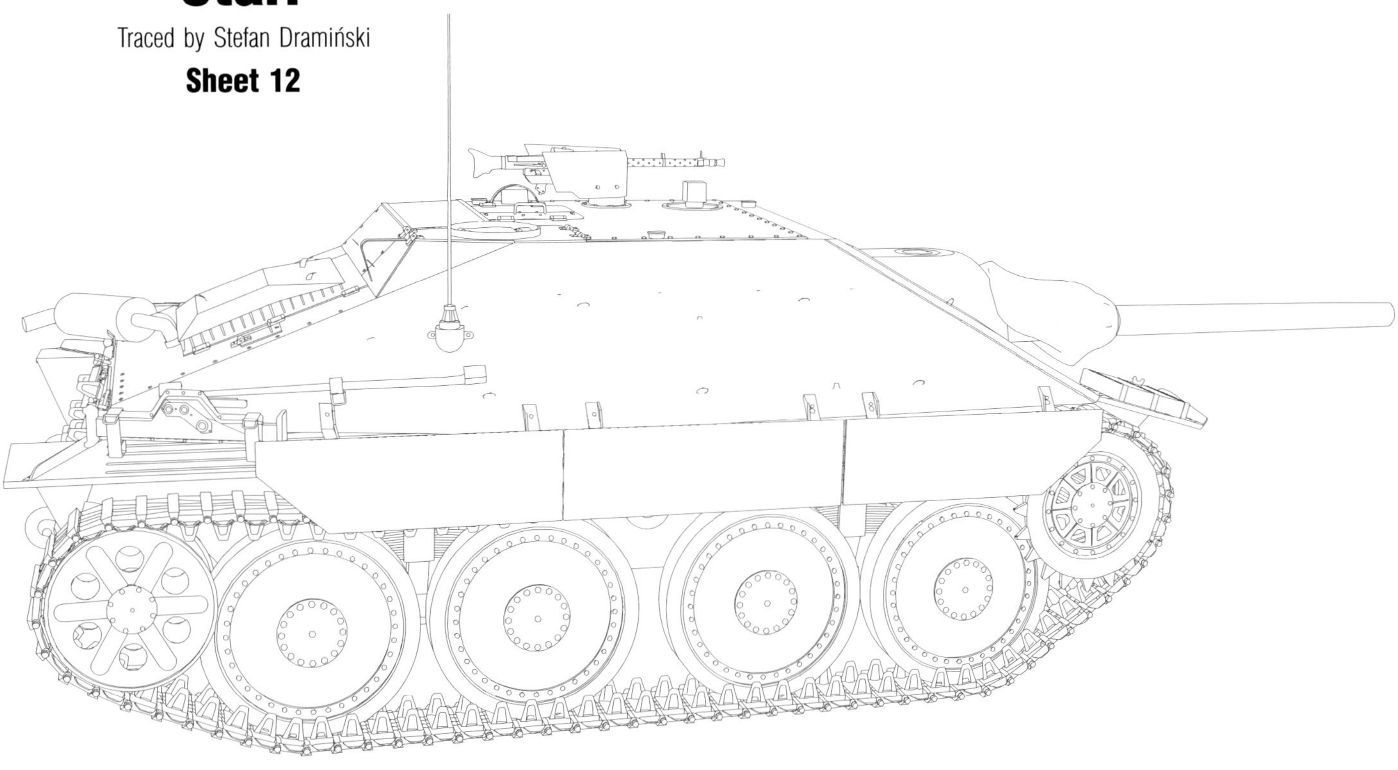

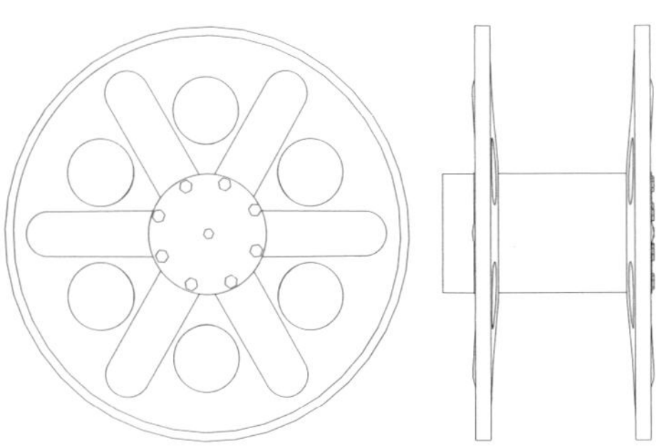

KAGERO

0 0,5 1 m

1/16 scale

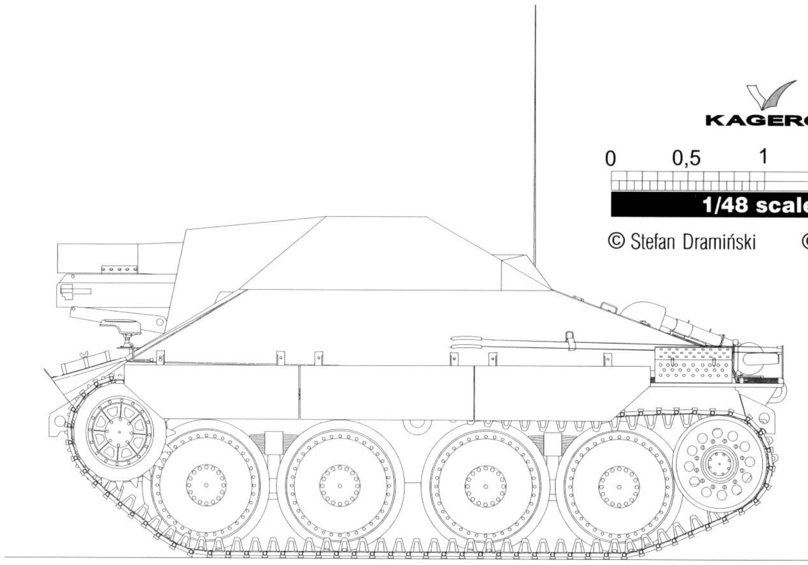

0 0,5 1 2 m

1/48 scale



# sIG 33/2 auf Jagdpanzer 38

Traced by Stefan Dramiński

**Sheet 13**

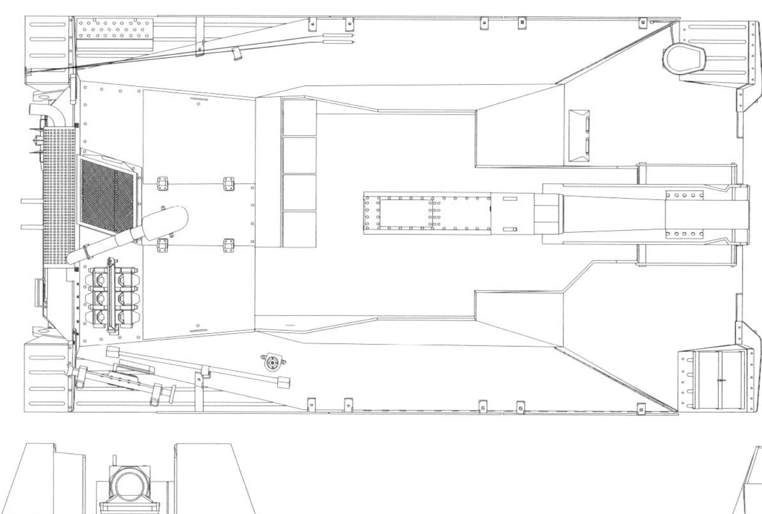

Details of the vehicle's interior omitted/

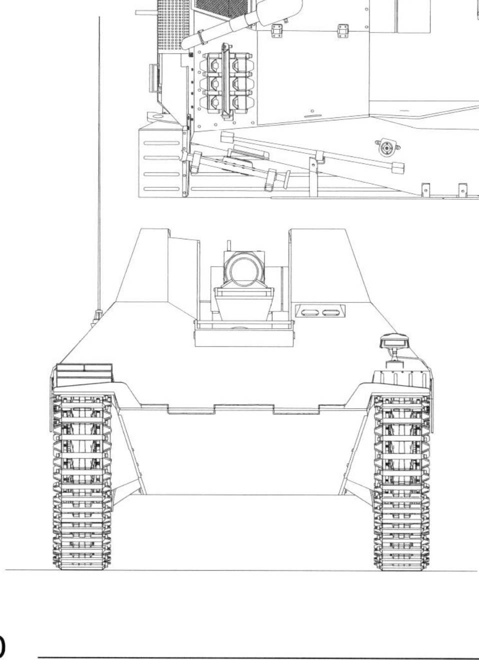

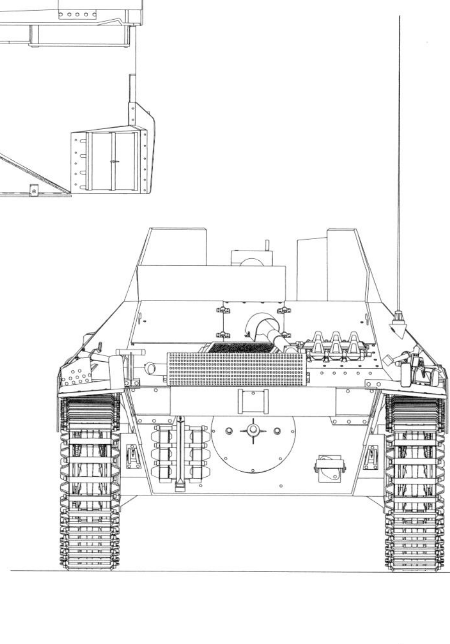

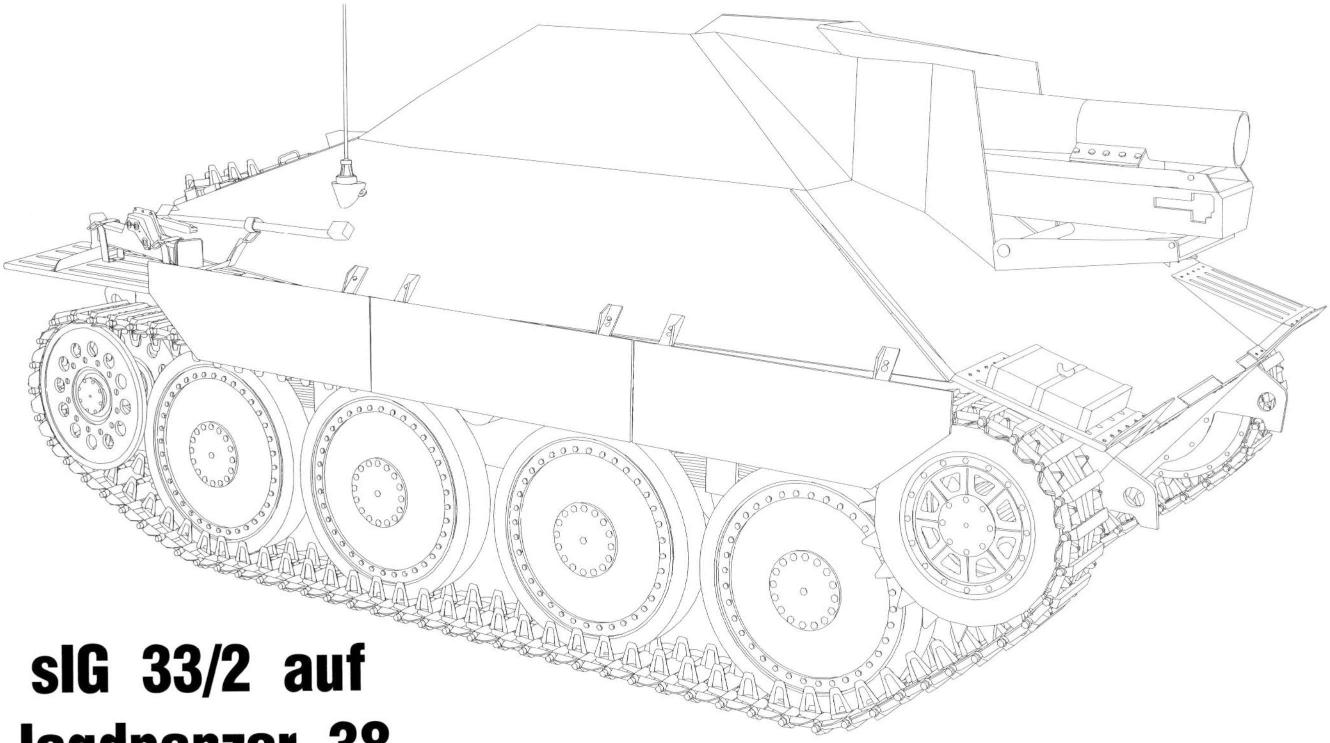

# sIG 33/2 auf Jagdpanzer 38

Traced by Stefan Dramiński

**Sheet 14**

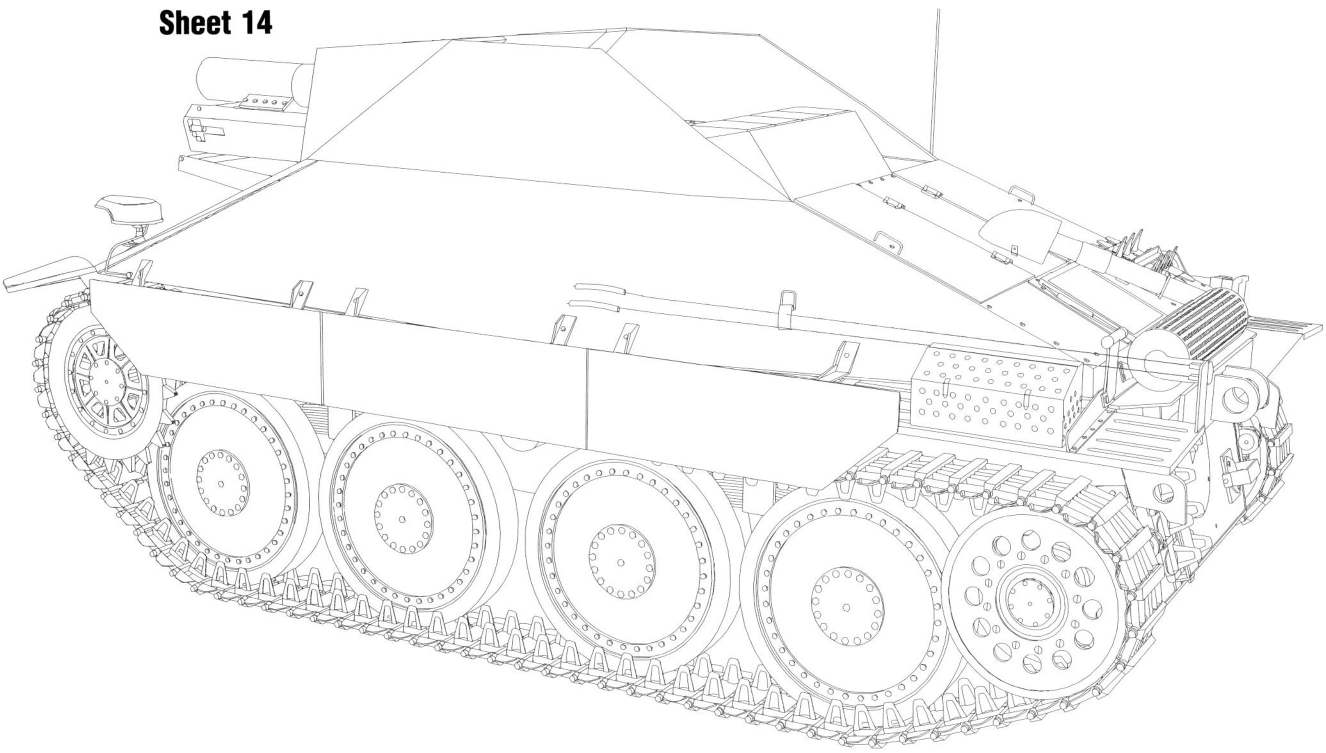

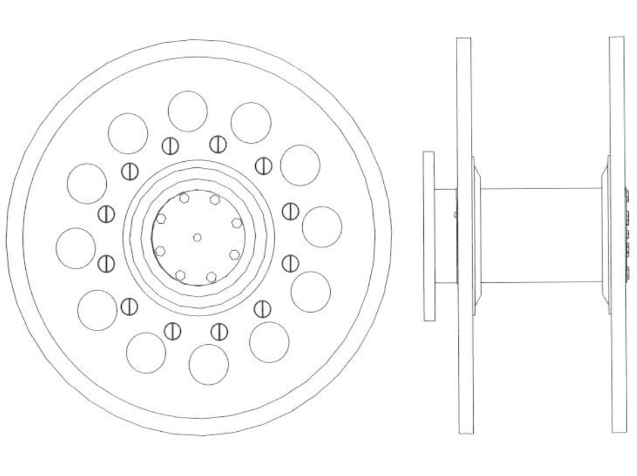

0 0,5 1 m

1/16 scale

KAGERO

0 0,5 1 2 m

1/48 scale



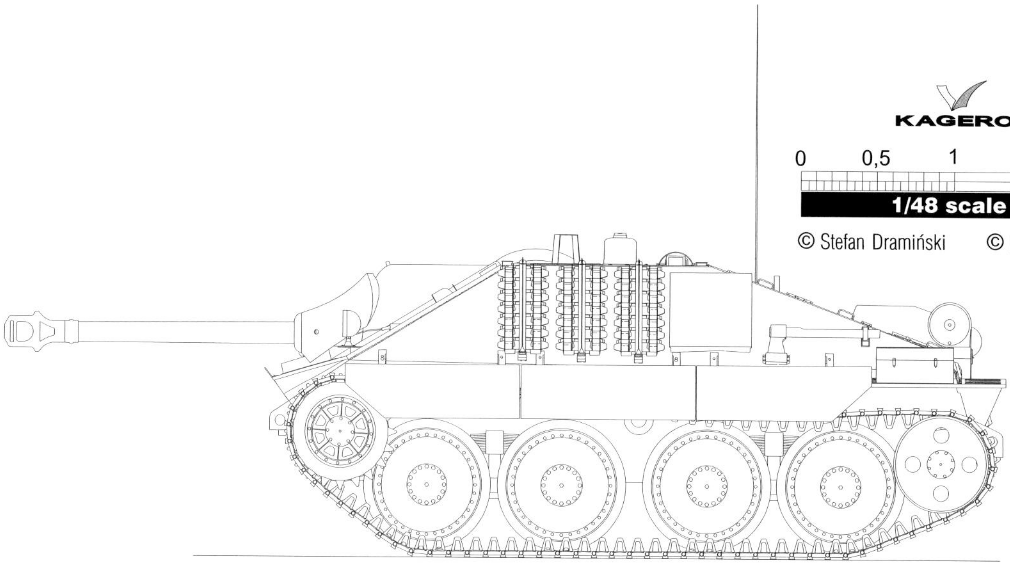

# G-13

Traced by Stefan Dramiński

**Sheet 15**

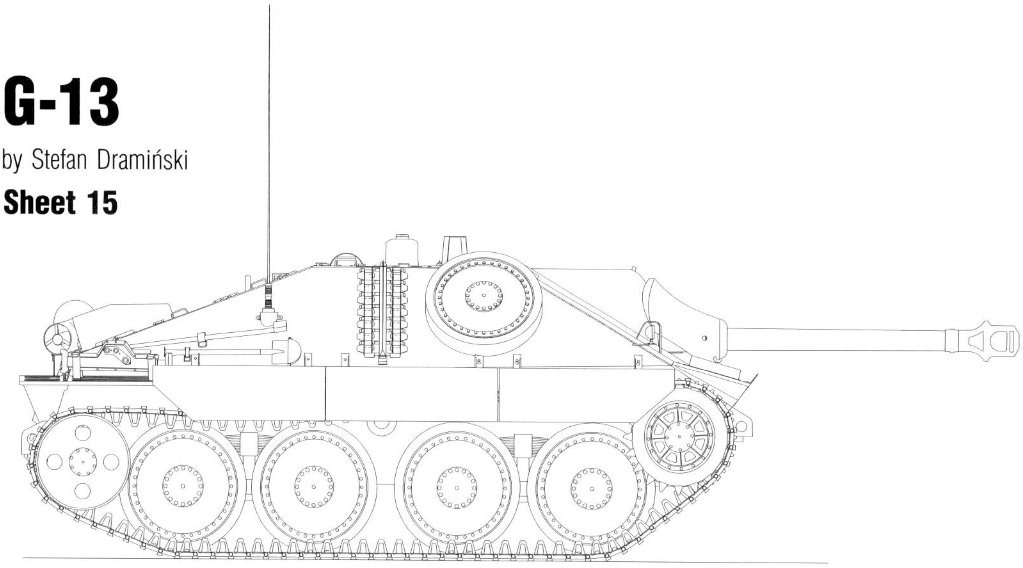

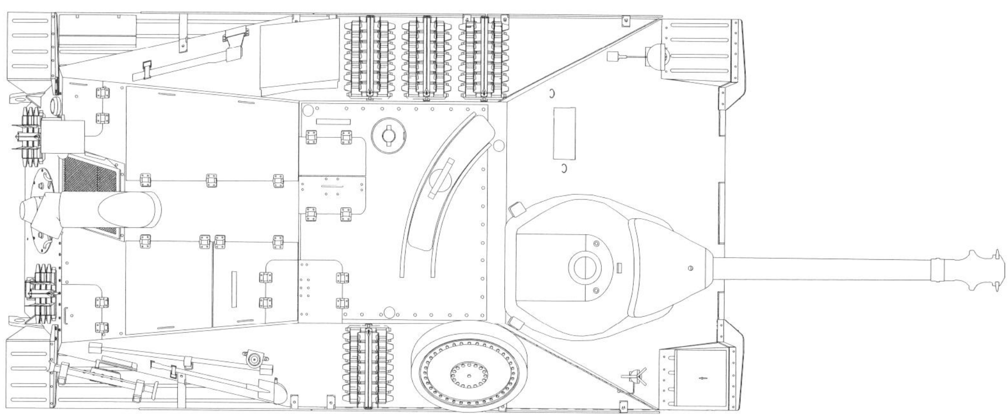

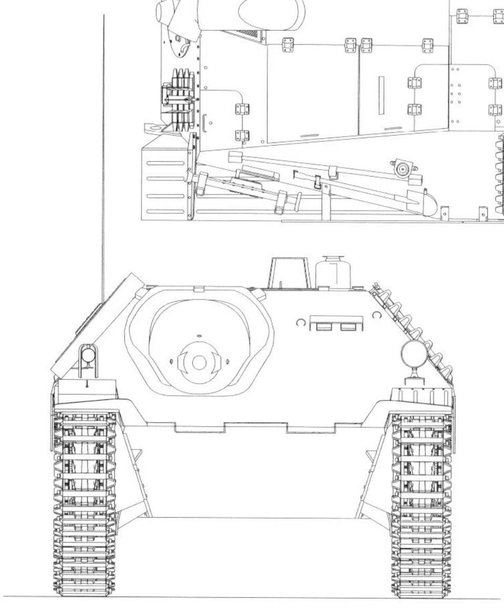

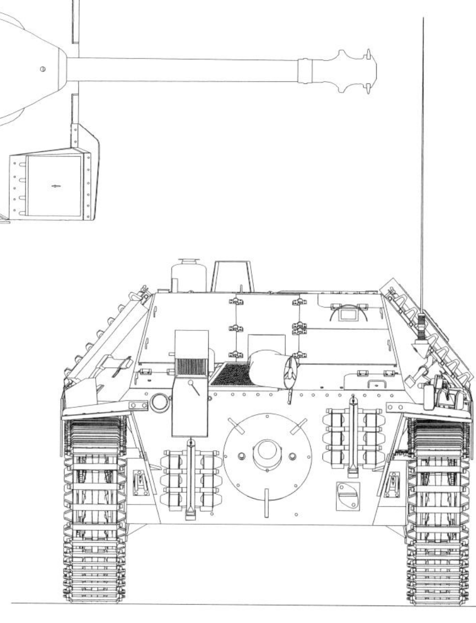

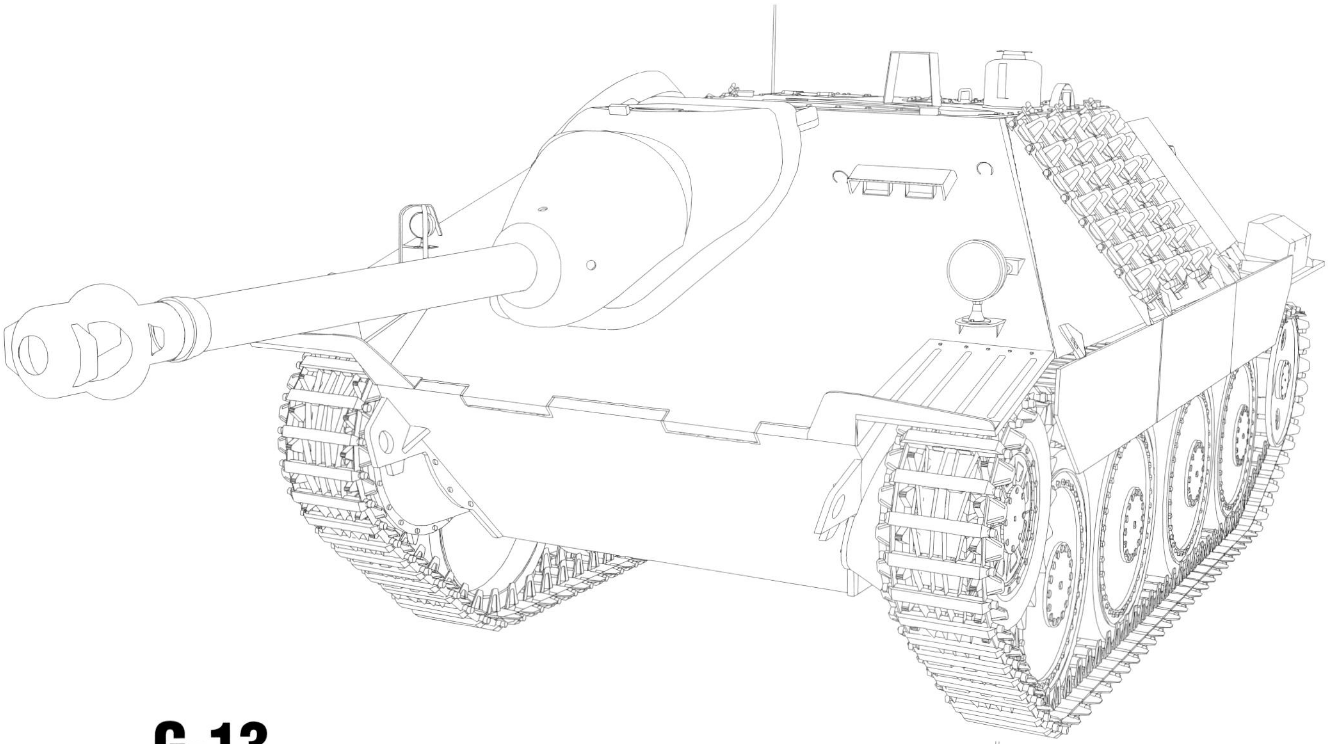

# G-13

Traced by Stefan Dramiński

**Sheet 16**

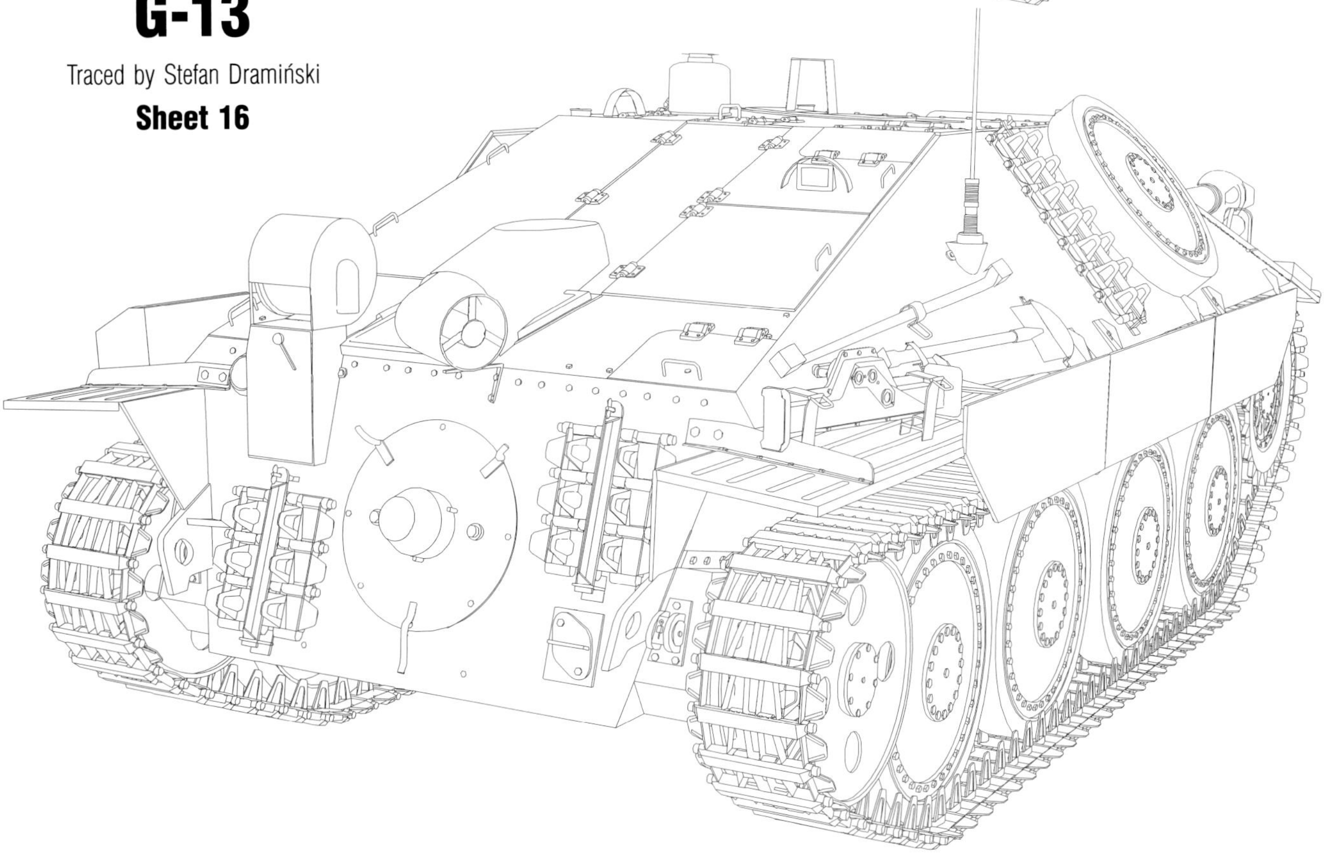

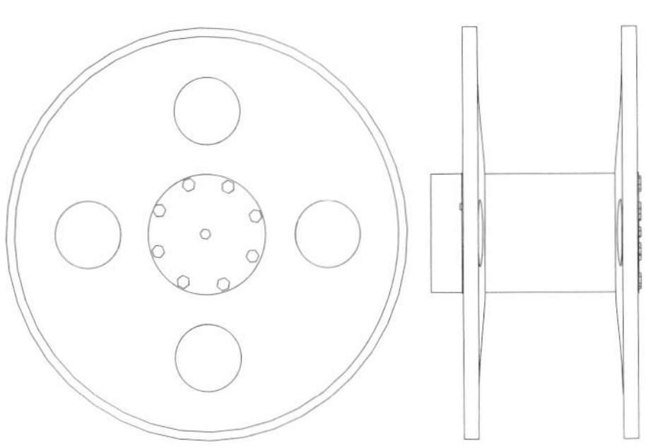

KAGERO

0 0,5 1 m

1/16 scale

Two shots of restored G-13, which external details are almost the same as in original Hetzer had. The vehicle is owned by 2nd Armored Productions from Clarksville, Indiana, USA. [Mike Koenig 2003, also credit 2nd Armored Productions, Clarksville, Indiana, USA]

Right side of G-13, rear part. Jack and other external equipment is clearly visible. [Mike Koenig 2001]

One more shot of Clarksville exhibit. This vehicle is not thrown open to public. [Mike Koenig 2001]

Close view of the driver's twin periscope protected by steel hood. [Mike Koenig 2003]

Gun yoke top view. Welds of armored plates are clearly visible. [Mike Koenig 2003, also credit 2nd Armored Productions]

Guide bar and movable gun periscope cover. [Mike Koenig 2003, also credit 2nd Armored Productions]

Rifling of the main gun barrel Stuk 40, 75 mm caliber. Original Hetzer had Pak 39 L/48, 75 mm cal gun. [Mike Koenig 2003]

Saukopf type gun yoke seen from the right. Wooden jack base on the foreground. [Mike Koenig 2003]

Numbering and lettering of the vehicle are not original, they were painted at 2nd Armored Productions. Note welded and interlocked arrmor plates. [Mike Koenig 2003]

Number 31 stamped in front armor plate. Meaning unknown. [Mike Koenig 2003]

Next shot of cover and periscope. [Mike Koenig 2003]

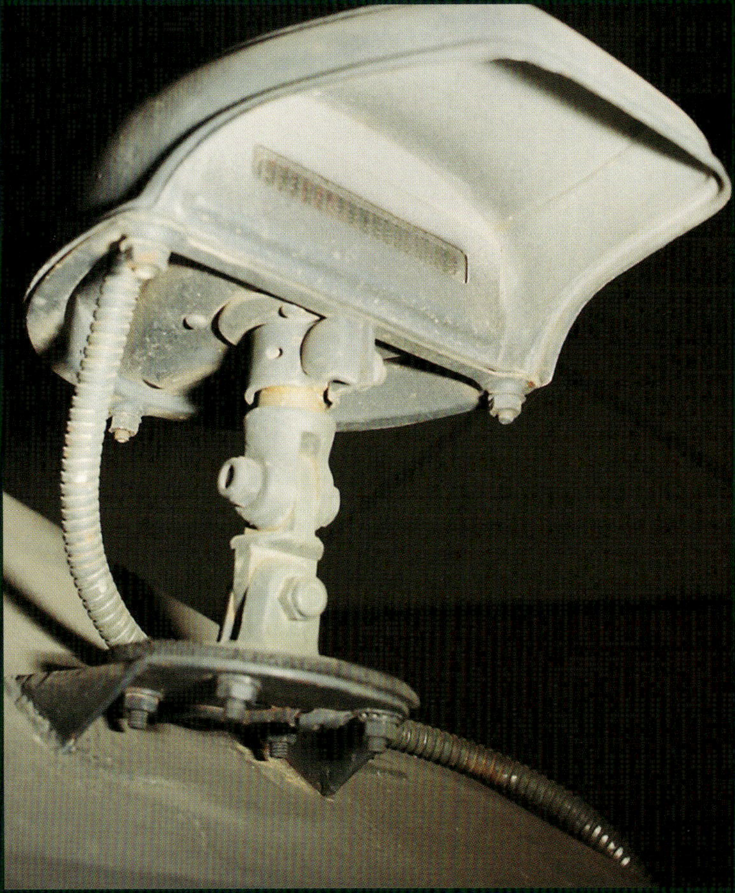
Notek light installed above the lef fender. [Mike Koenig 2003]

Pressed metal front fender, Notek lamp base, electric wire. [Mike Koenig]

Mount of remote controlled MG 34 in open position (upper and lower left photo) and shield of drive wheel on the right side of vehicle with visible oil valve. [Mike Koenig 2003, also credit 2nd Armored Productions]

Side plate with mounts of side shields of driving system. [Mike Koenig 2003]

Rear left fender with bracket and jack. Track adjustment fitting. [Mike Koenig 2003]

Rear view of bottom engine plate with towing cable, spare tracks and convoy light. Early type lamp not being mounted in Hetzers. Note starting crank shield. [Mike Koenig 2003]

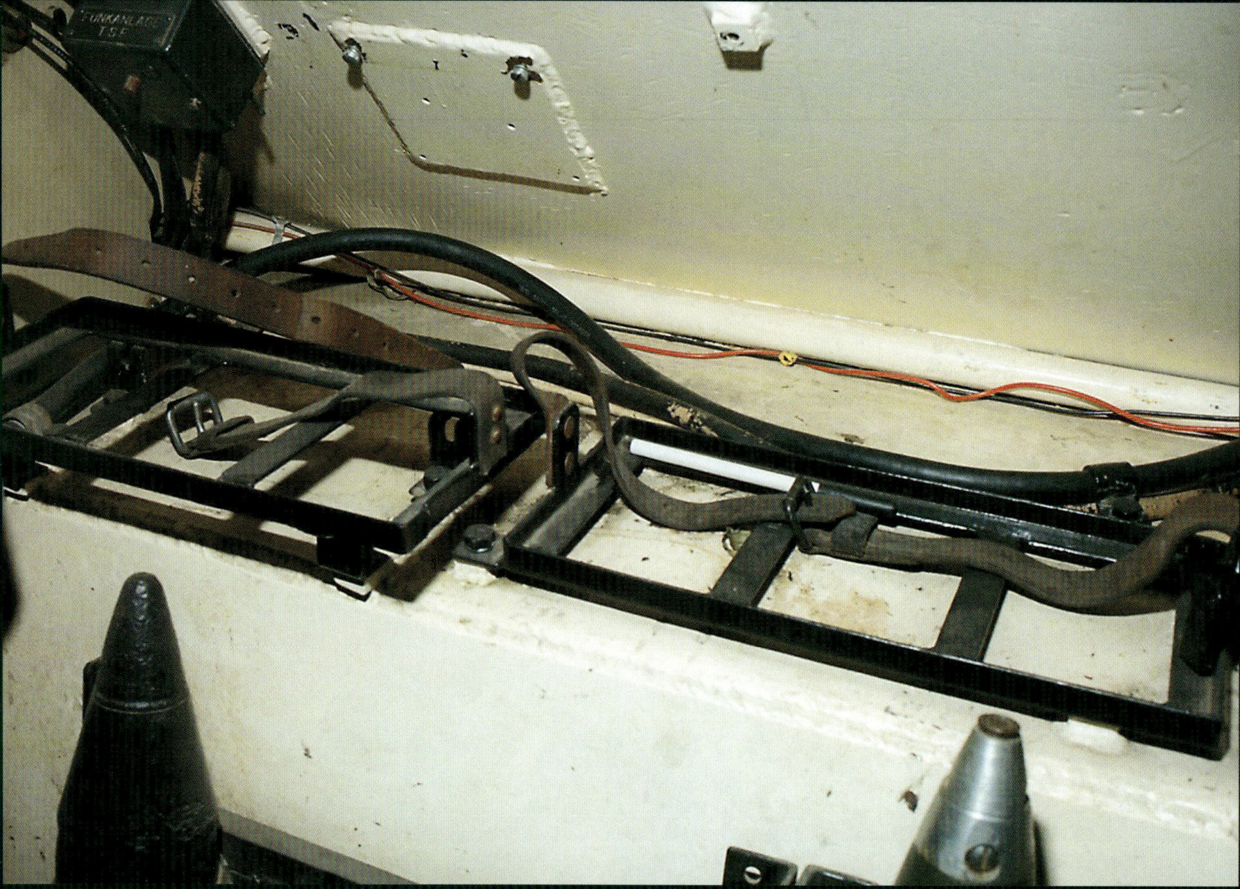

Radio holder and 75 mm ammo fastening on left side of crew compartment. [Mike Koenig 2003, also credit 2nd Armored Productions]

Rear view of crew compartment with visible gunner's and loeader's seats. Driving shaft with visible container for MG 34 ammo. [Mike Koenig 2003]

Brake mechanism on left side of vehicle and two shots of driver's position. [Mike Koenig 2003, also credit 2nd Armored Productions]

Driver's position and close view of instrument panel and twin periscopes. [Mike Koenig 2003]

Interior of crew compartment with visible periscope mounted near MG controlled from interior. [Mike Koenig 2003]

Elements of driving system on this and next pages. [Mike Koenig 2003]

Suspension elements on this and next pages. [Mike Koenig 2003]

Painted by Mariusz Motyka

Jagdpanzer 38(t) Hetzer right sight cross-section. Main armament, a part of drive shaft and ammunition racks are clearly visible.

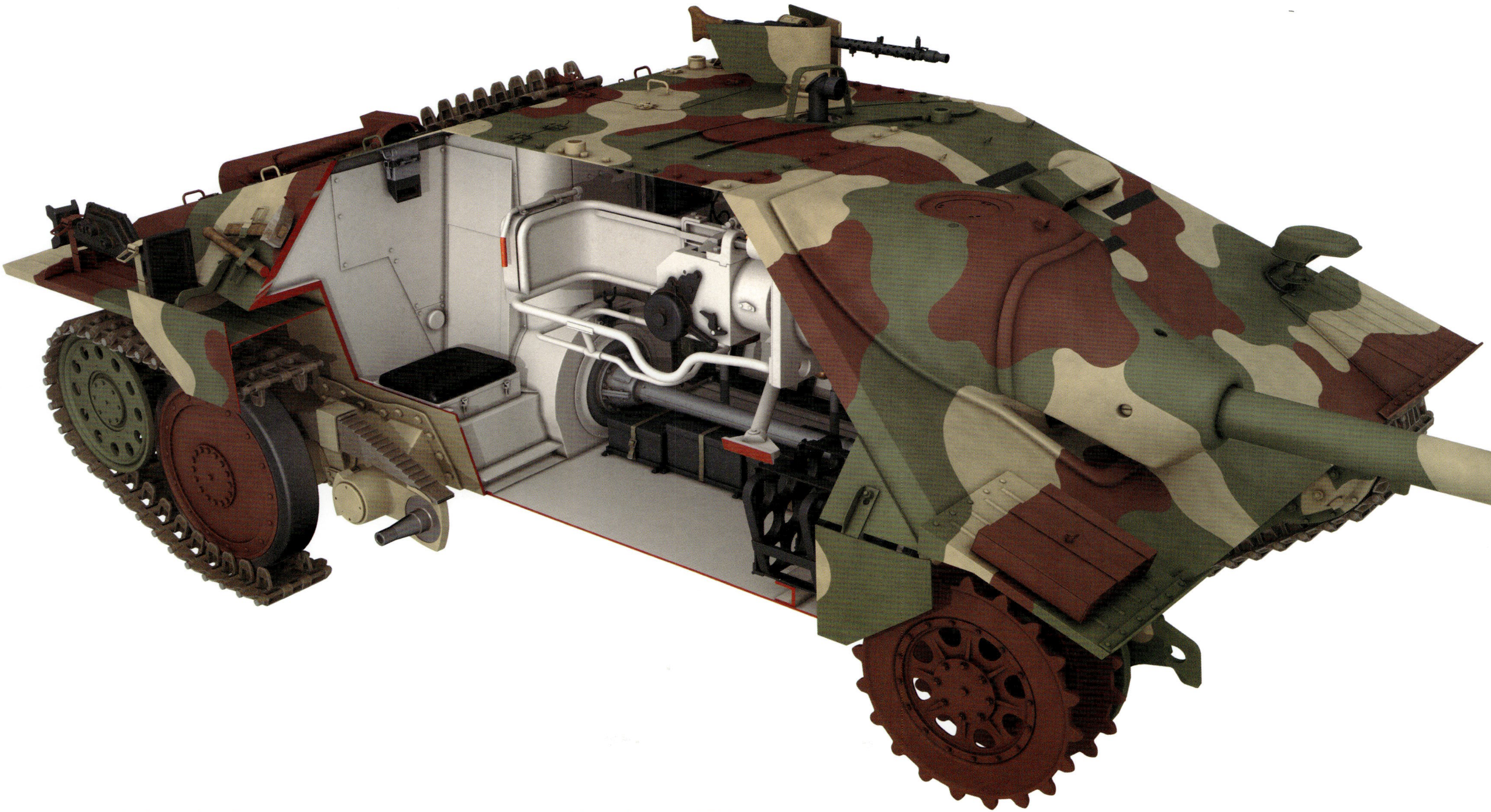

Jagdpanzer 38(t) Hetzer right upper view with a partly cross-section of the combat compartment.

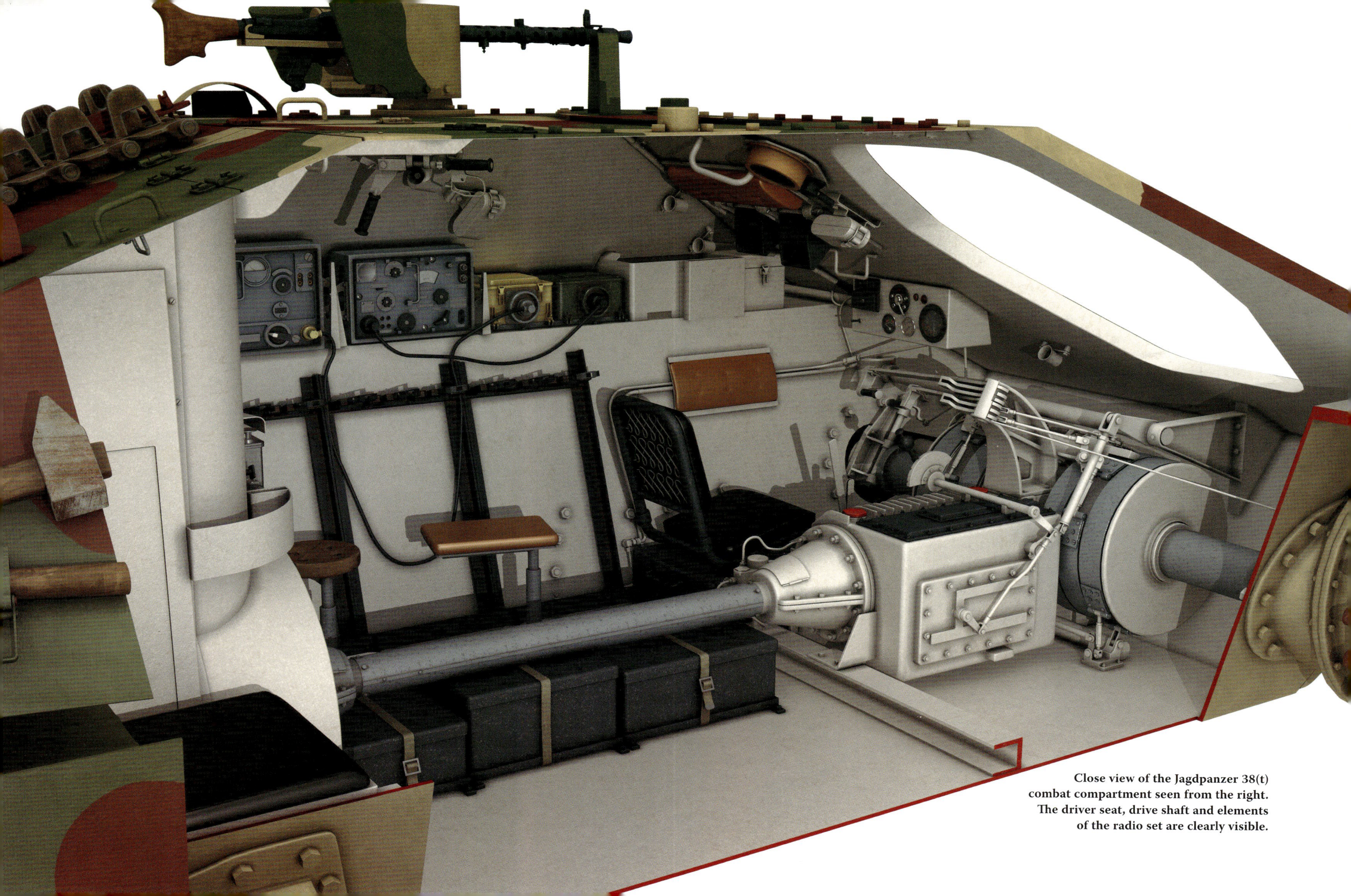

Close view of the Jagdpanzer 38(t) combat compartment seen from the right. The driver seat, drive shaft and elements of the radio set are clearly visible.

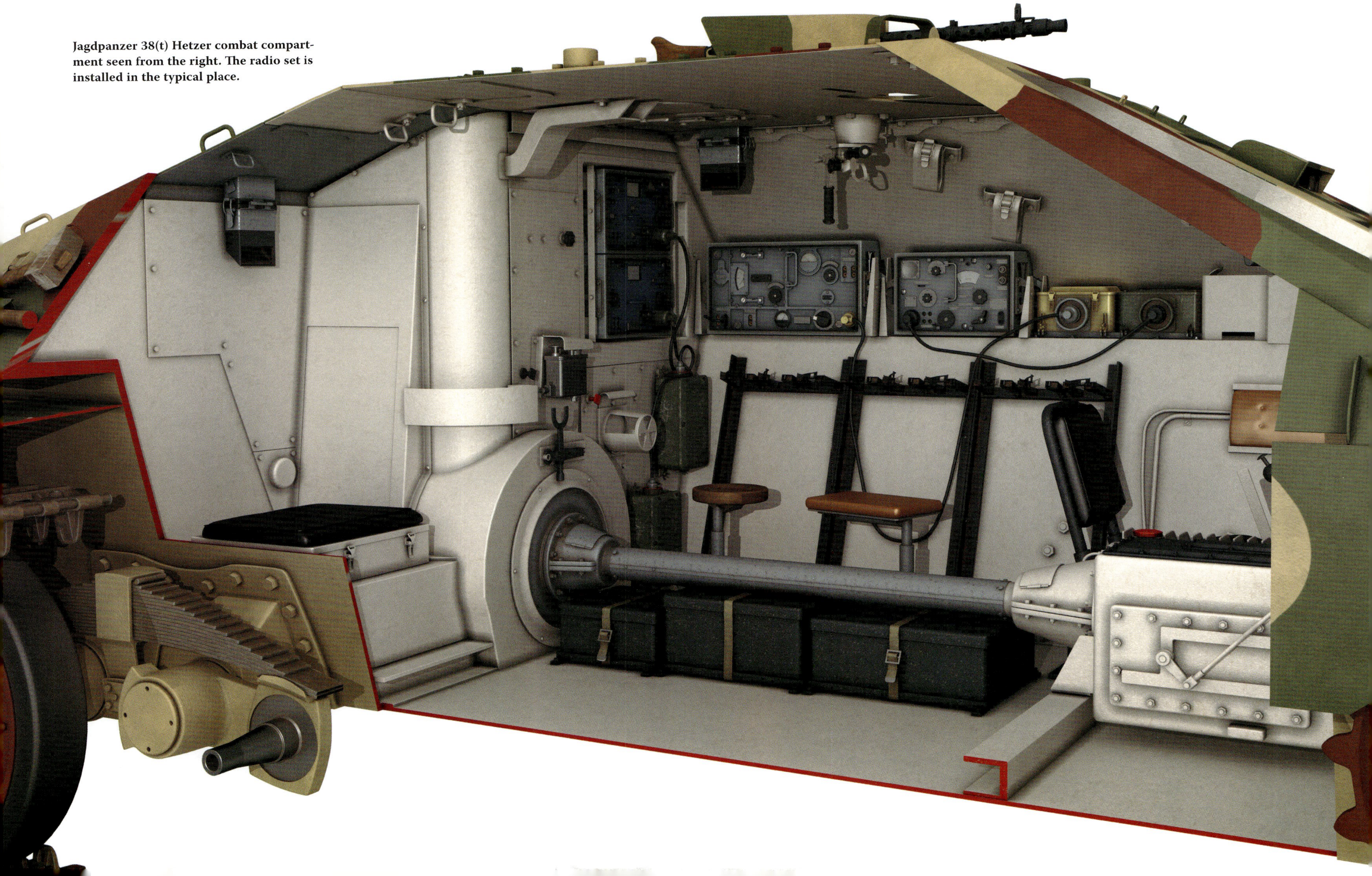

Jagdpanzer 38(t) Hetzer combat compartment seen from the right. The radio set is installed in the typical place.

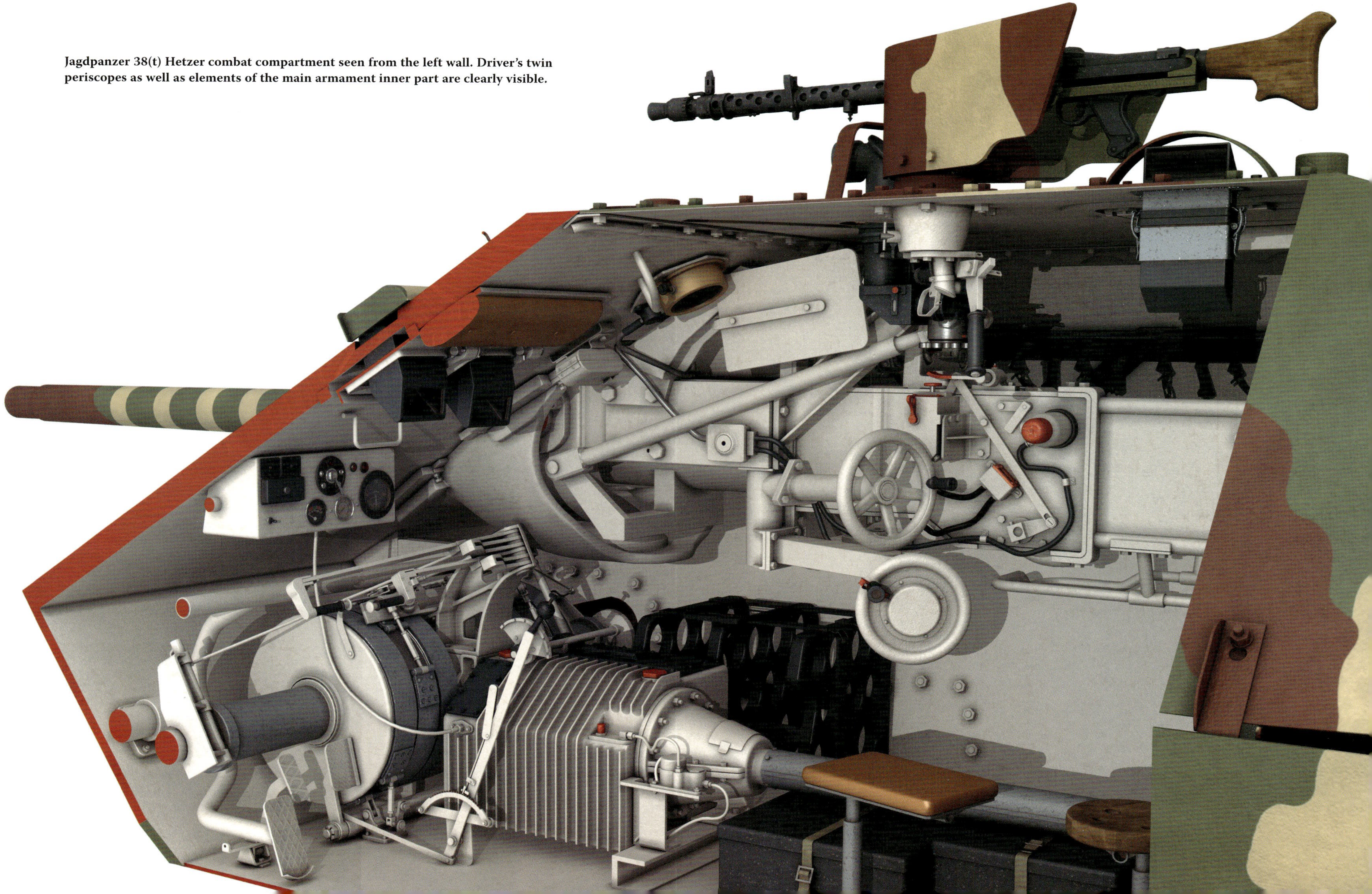

Jagdpanzer 38(t) Hetzer combat compartment seen from the left wall. Driver's twin periscopes as well as elements of the main armament inner part are clearly visible.

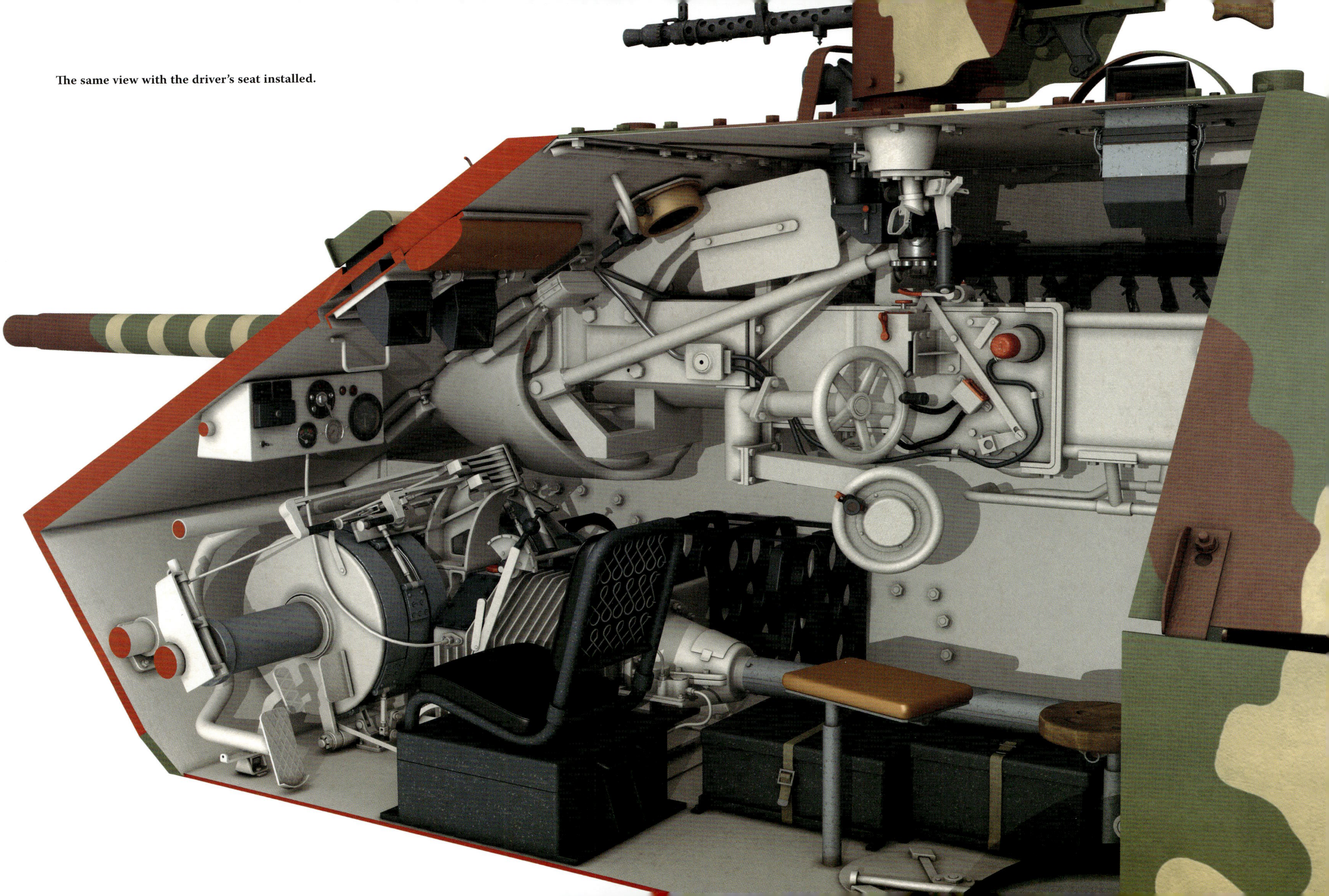

The same view with the driver's seat installed.

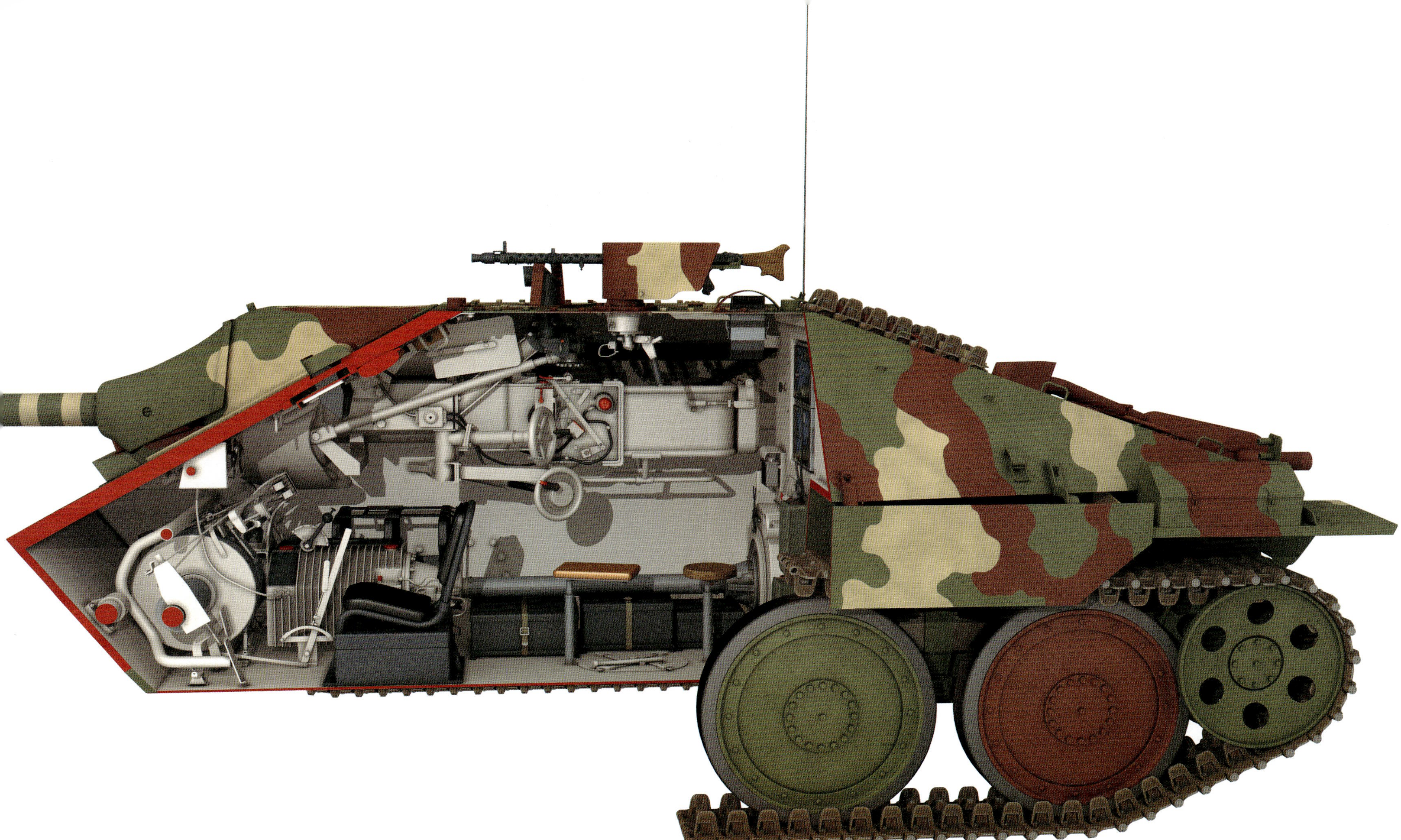

**Jagdpanzer 38(t) seen from the left with a combat compartment cross-section.**

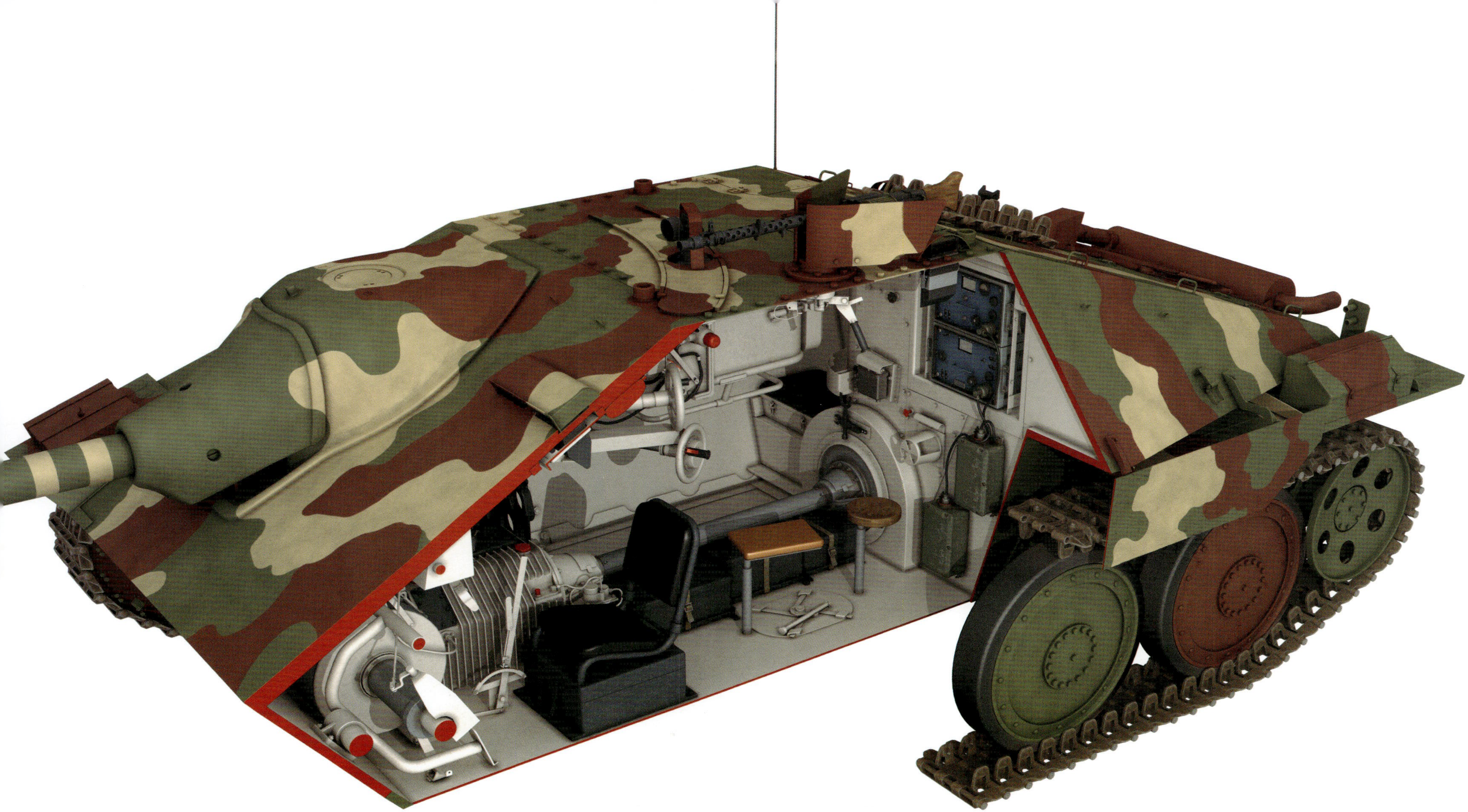

Jagdpanzer 38(t) seen from the left with a combat compartment cross-section.

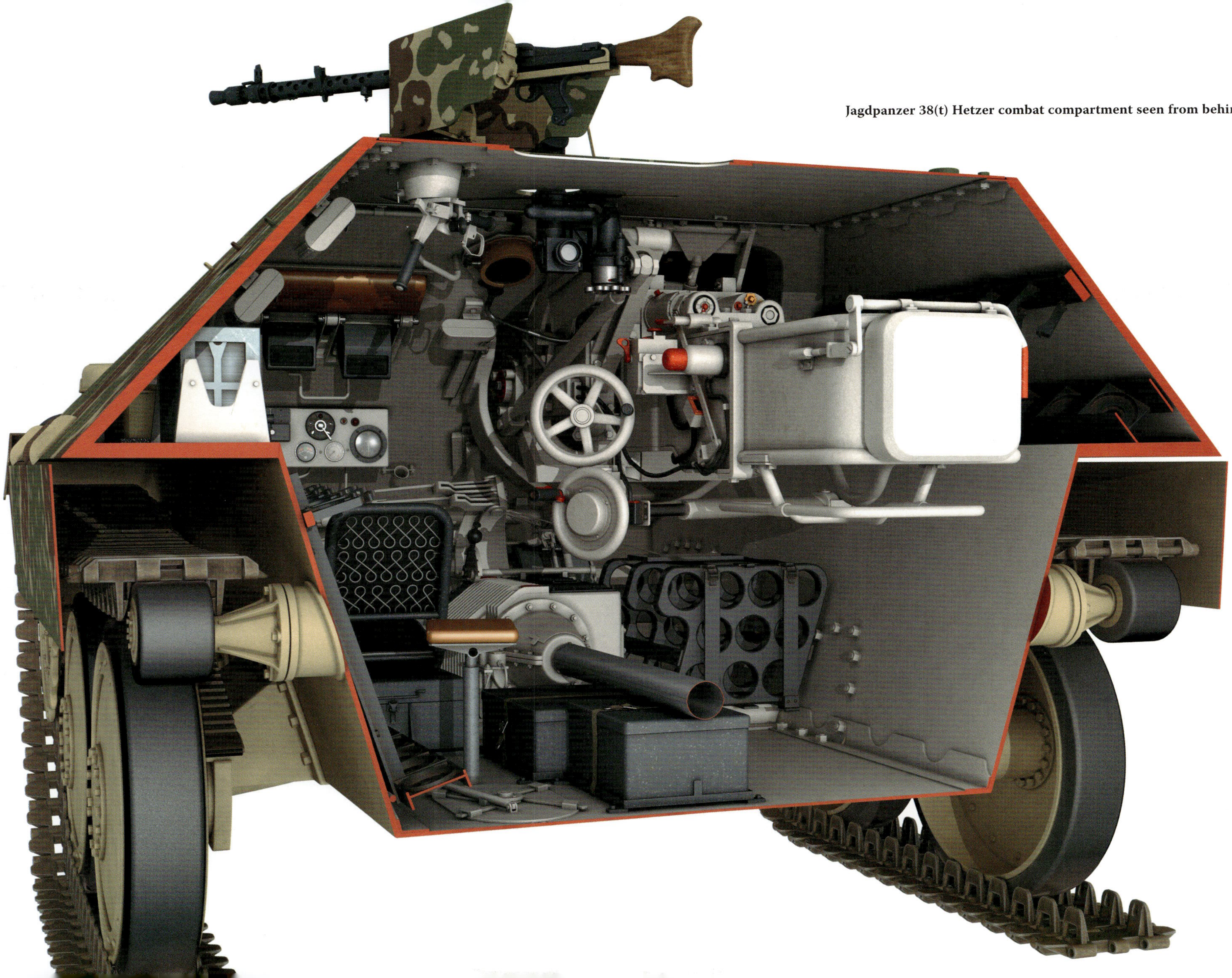

Jagdpanzer 38(t) Hetzer combat compartment seen from behind.

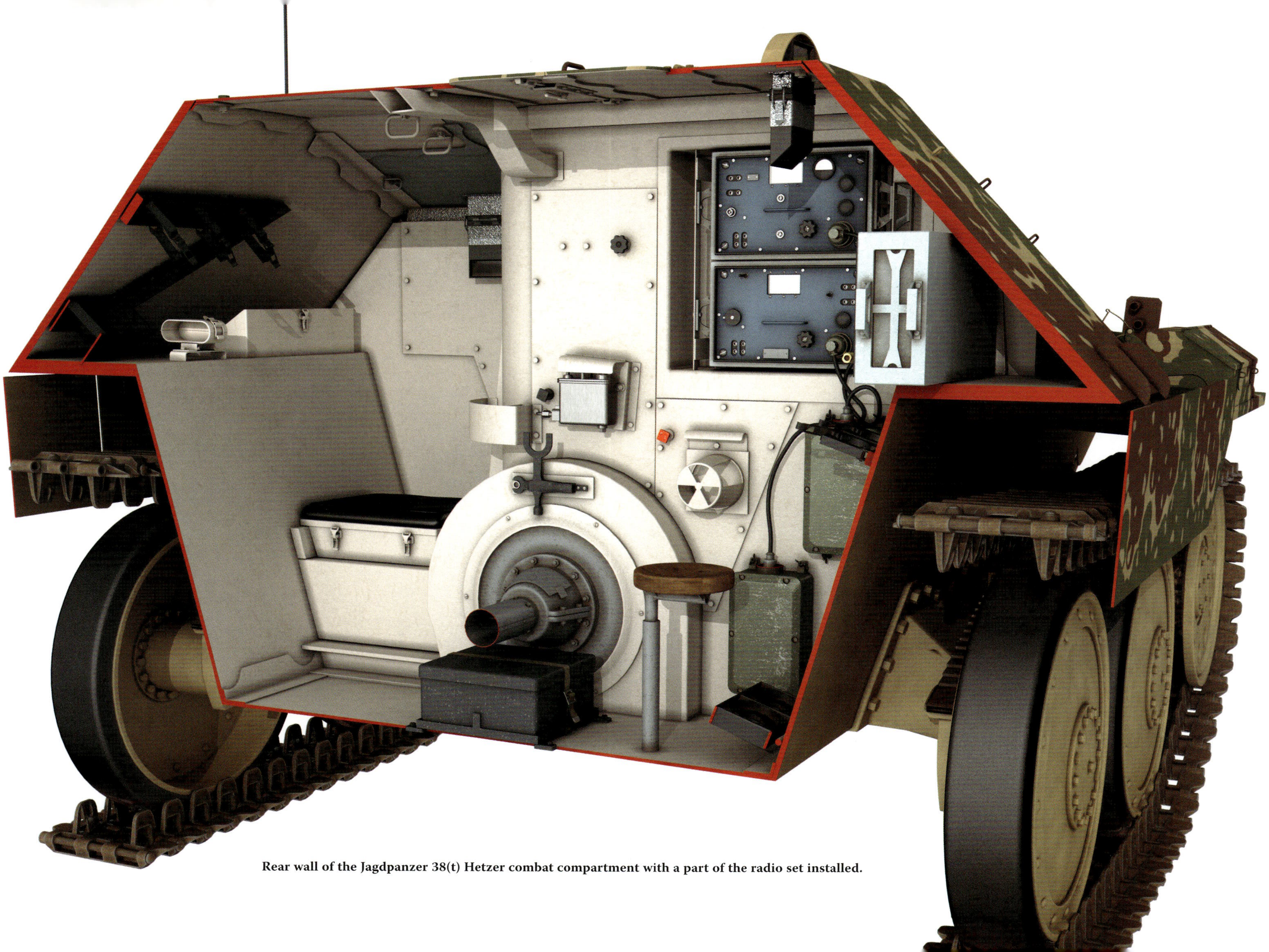

Rear wall of the Jagdpanzer 38(t) Hetzer combat compartment with a part of the radio set installed.

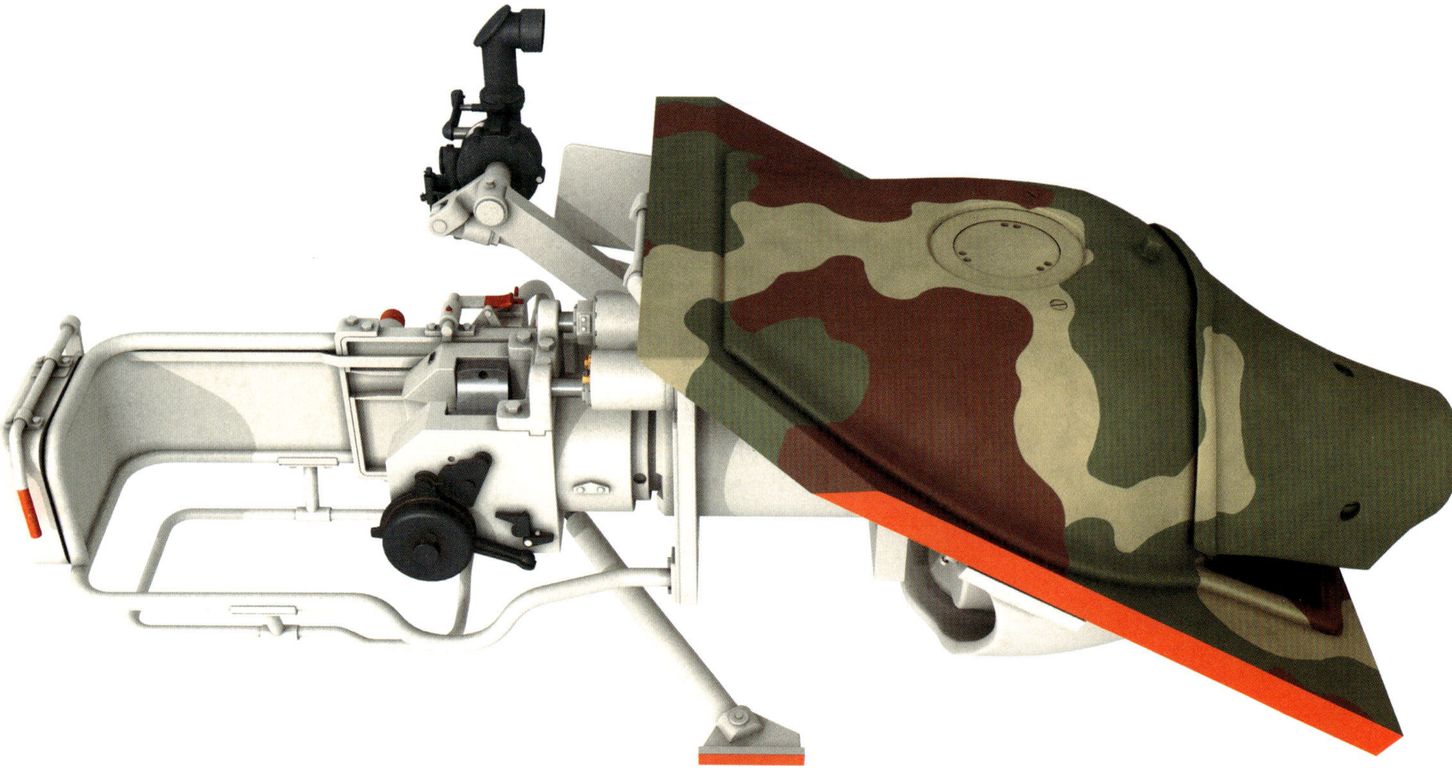

7,5 cm StuK 40 L/48 – the main armament installed in G-13 vehicles and probably in a part of late production series of Jagpanzer 38(t) Hetzer.

3D visualization of Jagdpanzer 38(t) Hetzer main armament – 7,5 cm PaK 39 gun will be presented in the second volume of this book.

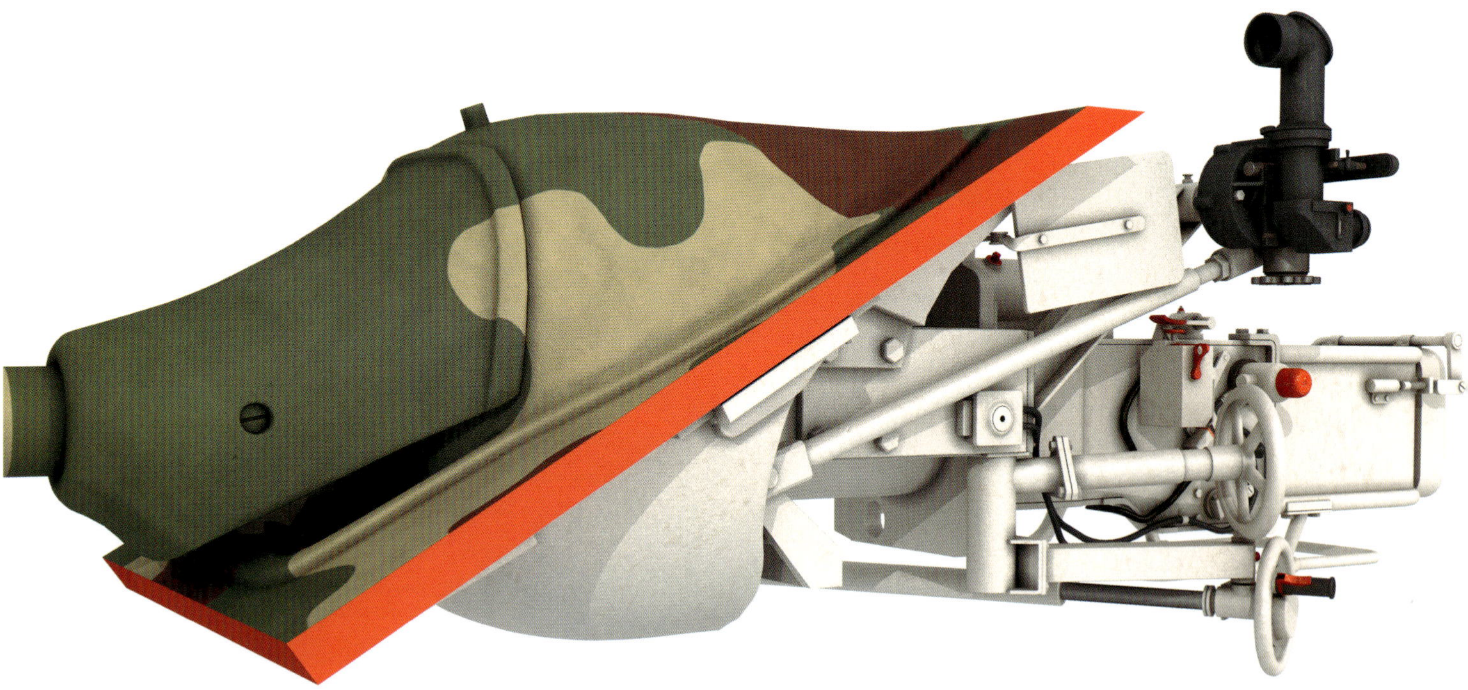

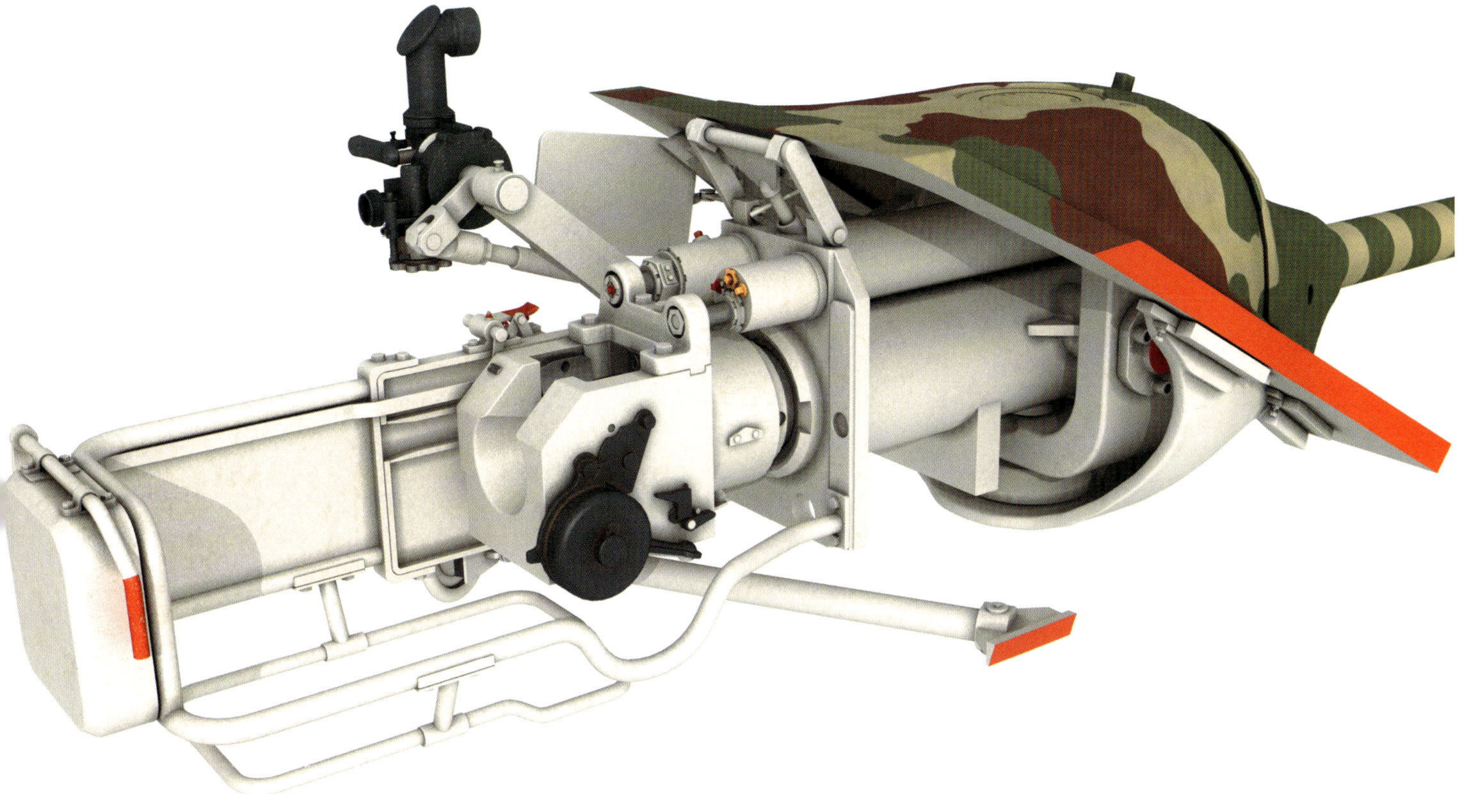

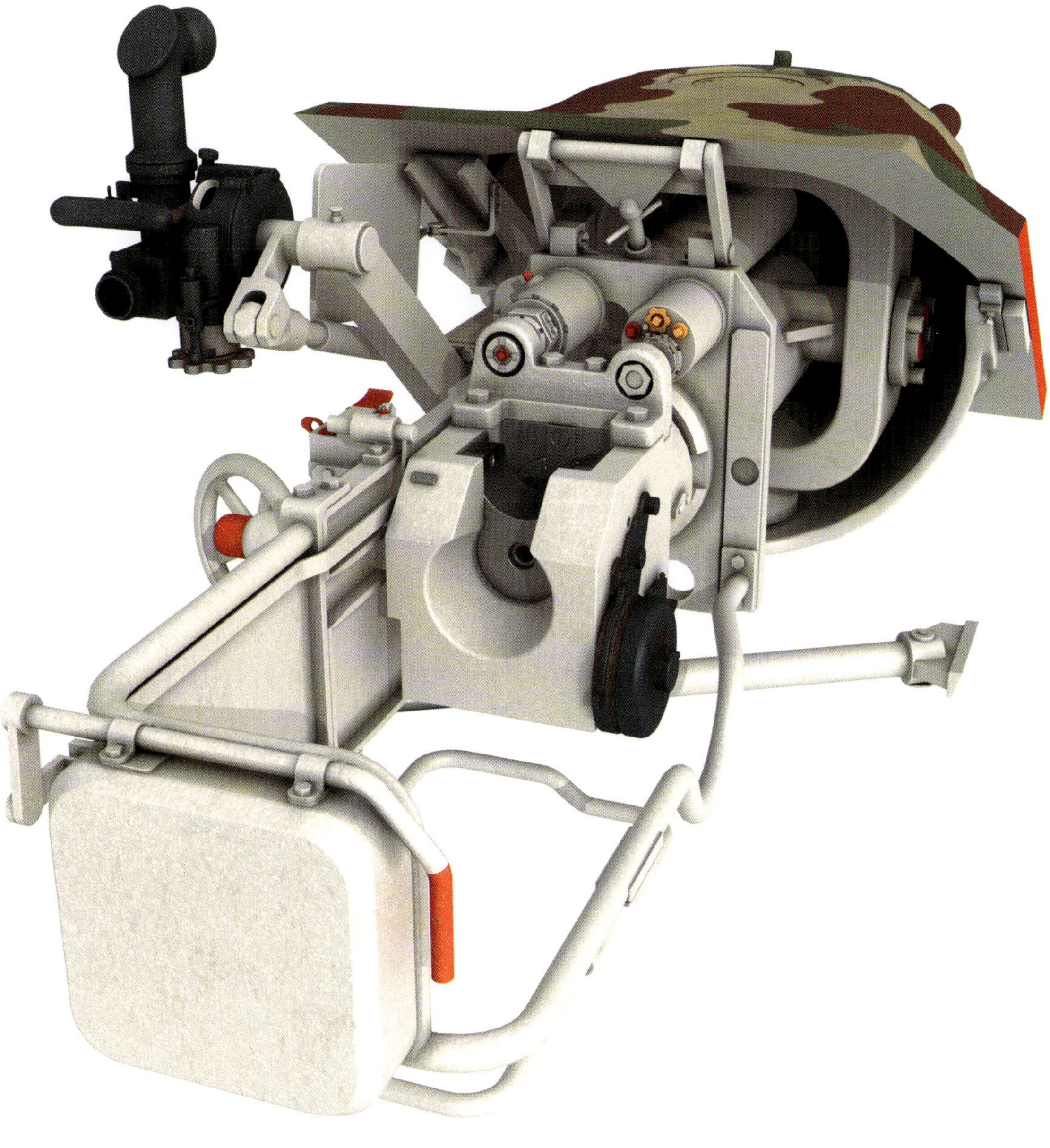

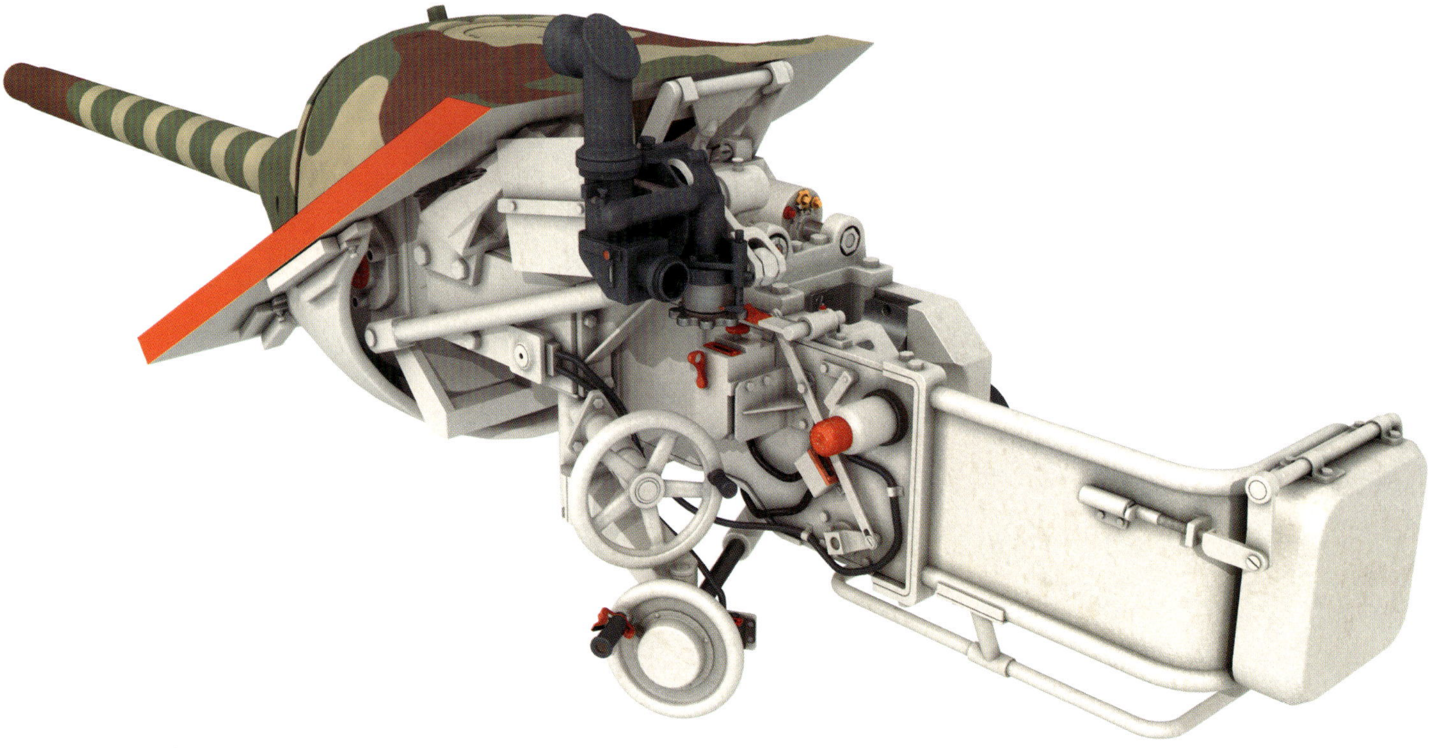

Left side of the 7,5 cm StuK 40 L/48 gun inner part. Adjustment dials and the lower part of the periscopic viewfinder are clearly visible.

Sfl ZF1a periscopic sight lower part details. ▲

10-watt FuG5 radio set usually installed in the Jagdpanzer 38(t) Hetzer. ▼

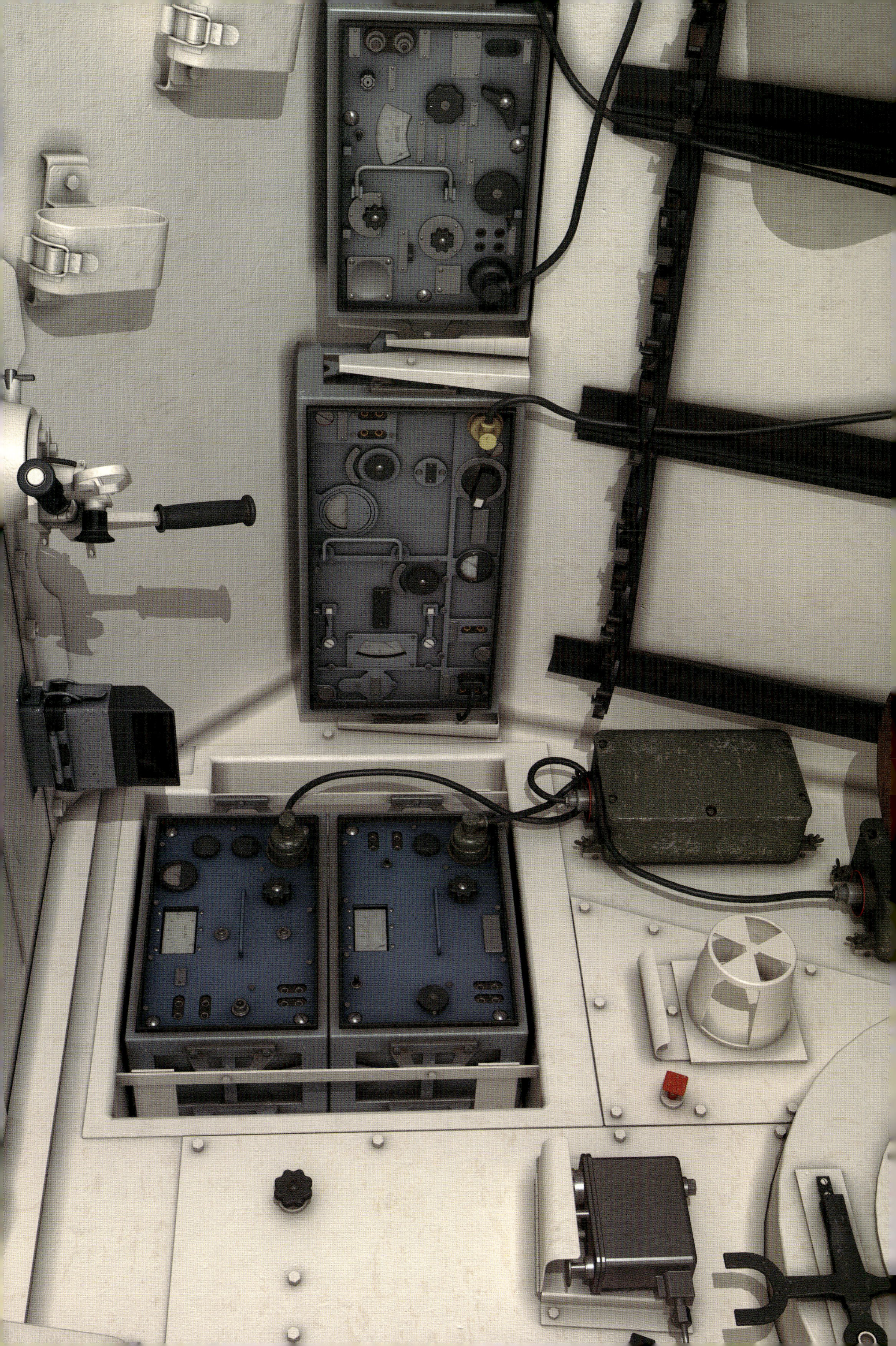

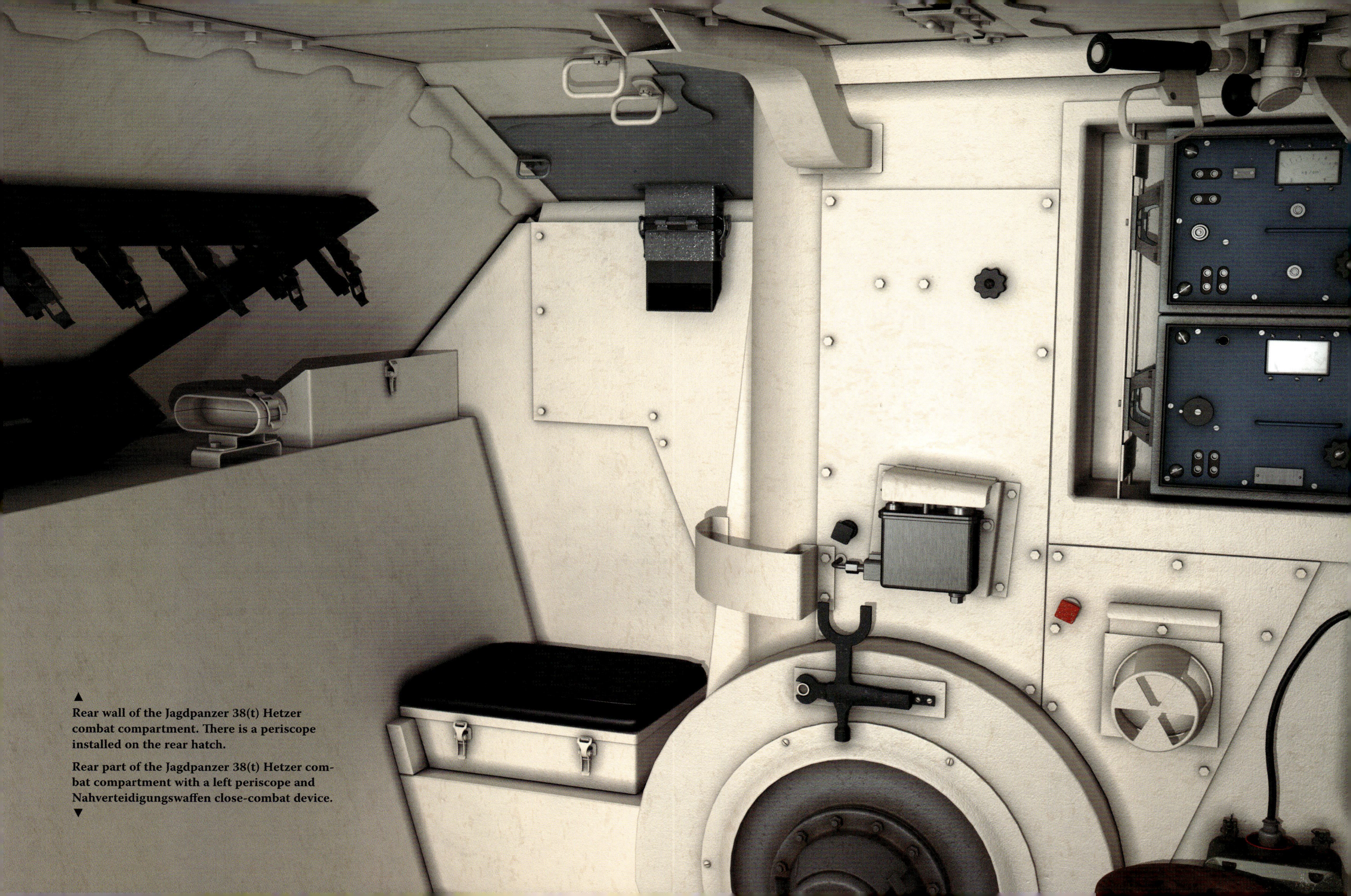

▲ Rear wall of the Jagdpanzer 38(t) Hetzer combat compartment. There is a periscope installed on the rear hatch.

Rear part of the Jagdpanzer 38(t) Hetzer combat compartment with a left periscope and Nahverteidigungswaffen close-combat device. ▼

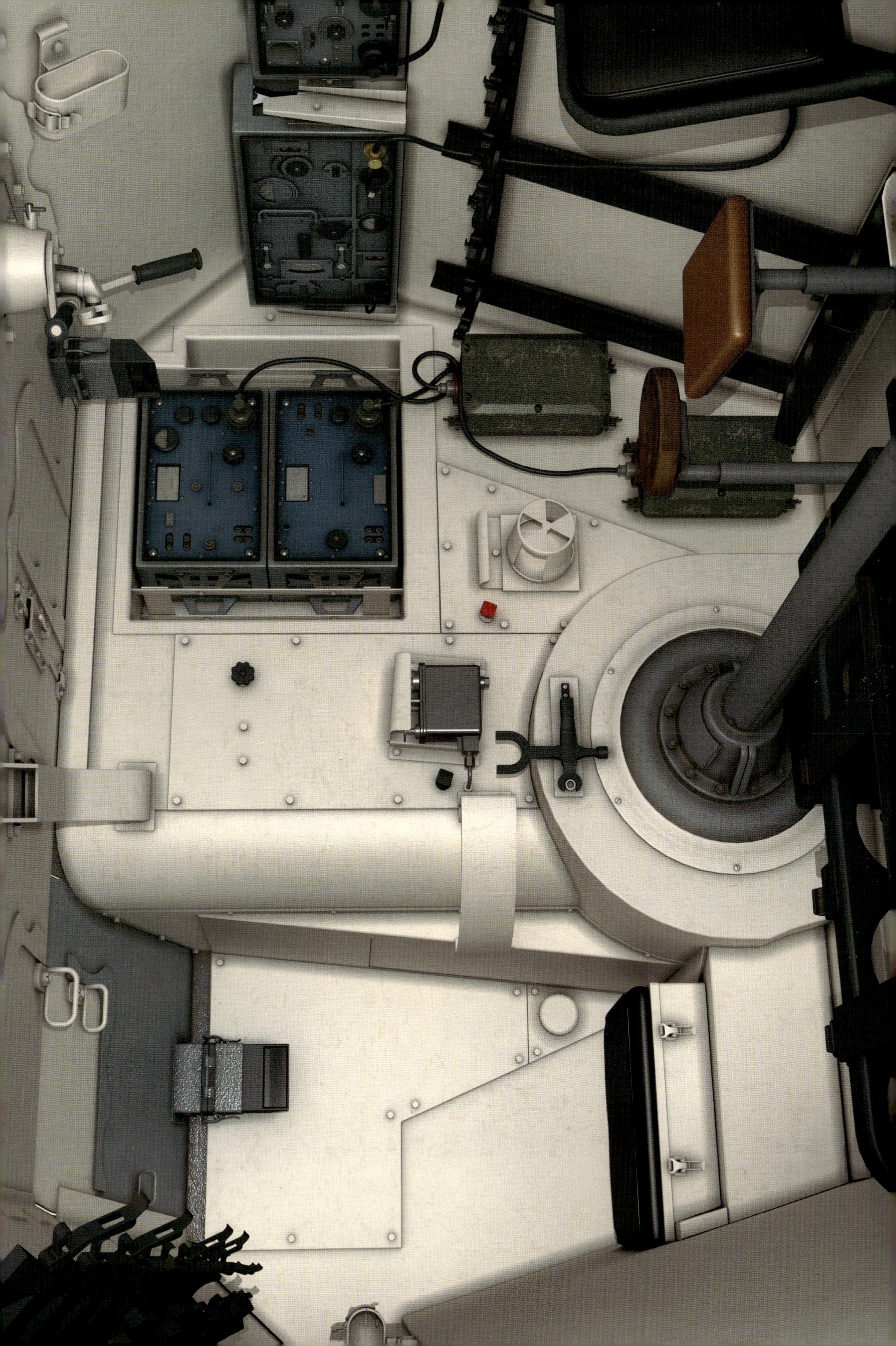

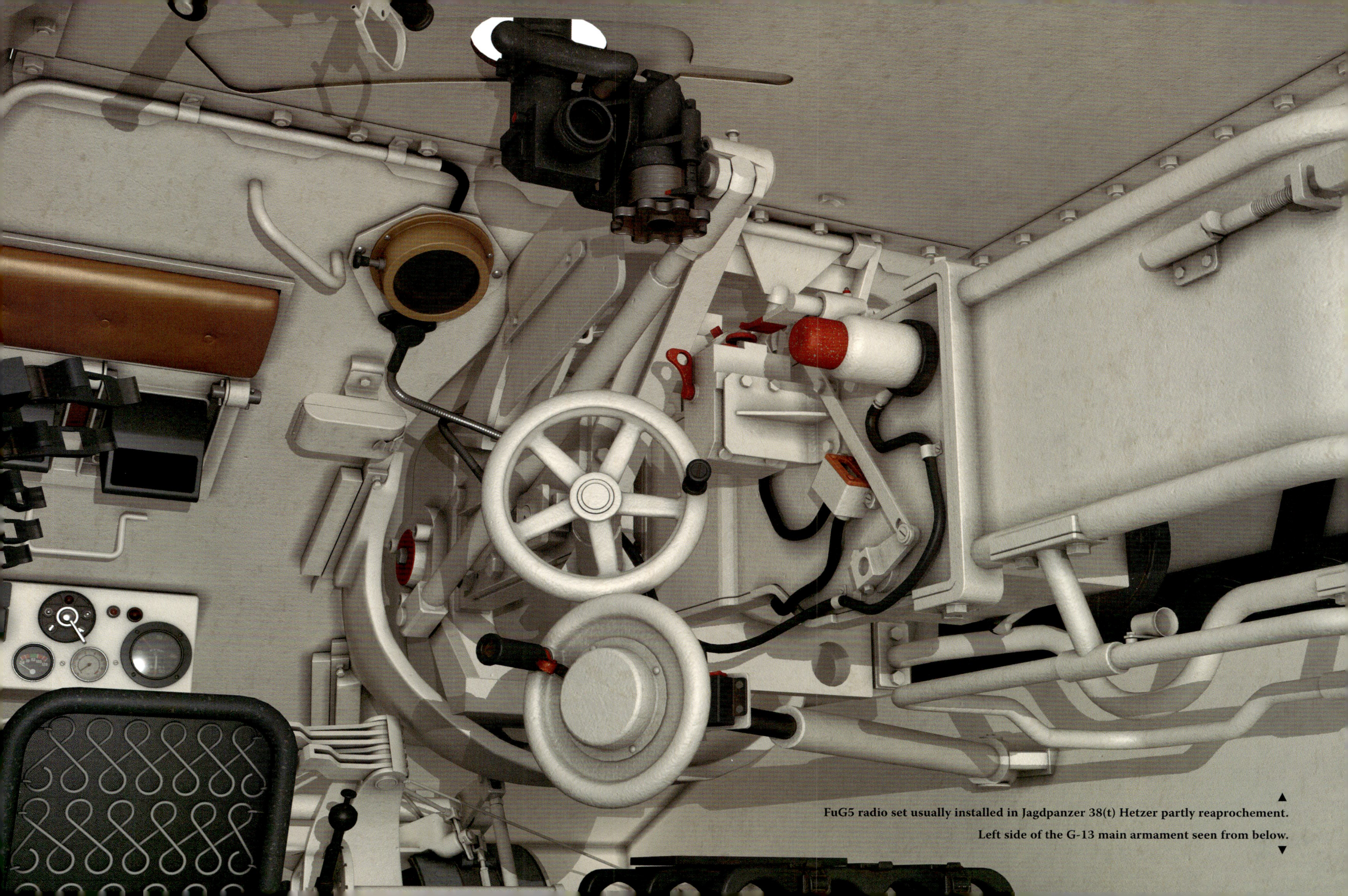

FuG5 radio set usually installed in Jagdpanzer 38(t) Hetzer partly reaprochement.

Left side of the G-13 main armament seen from below.

▲ 7,5 cm StuK 40 L/48 inner part seen from behind. The massive gun lock can be easily find.

7,5 cm Stuk 40 L/48 inner part seen from the vehicle commander seat. ▼

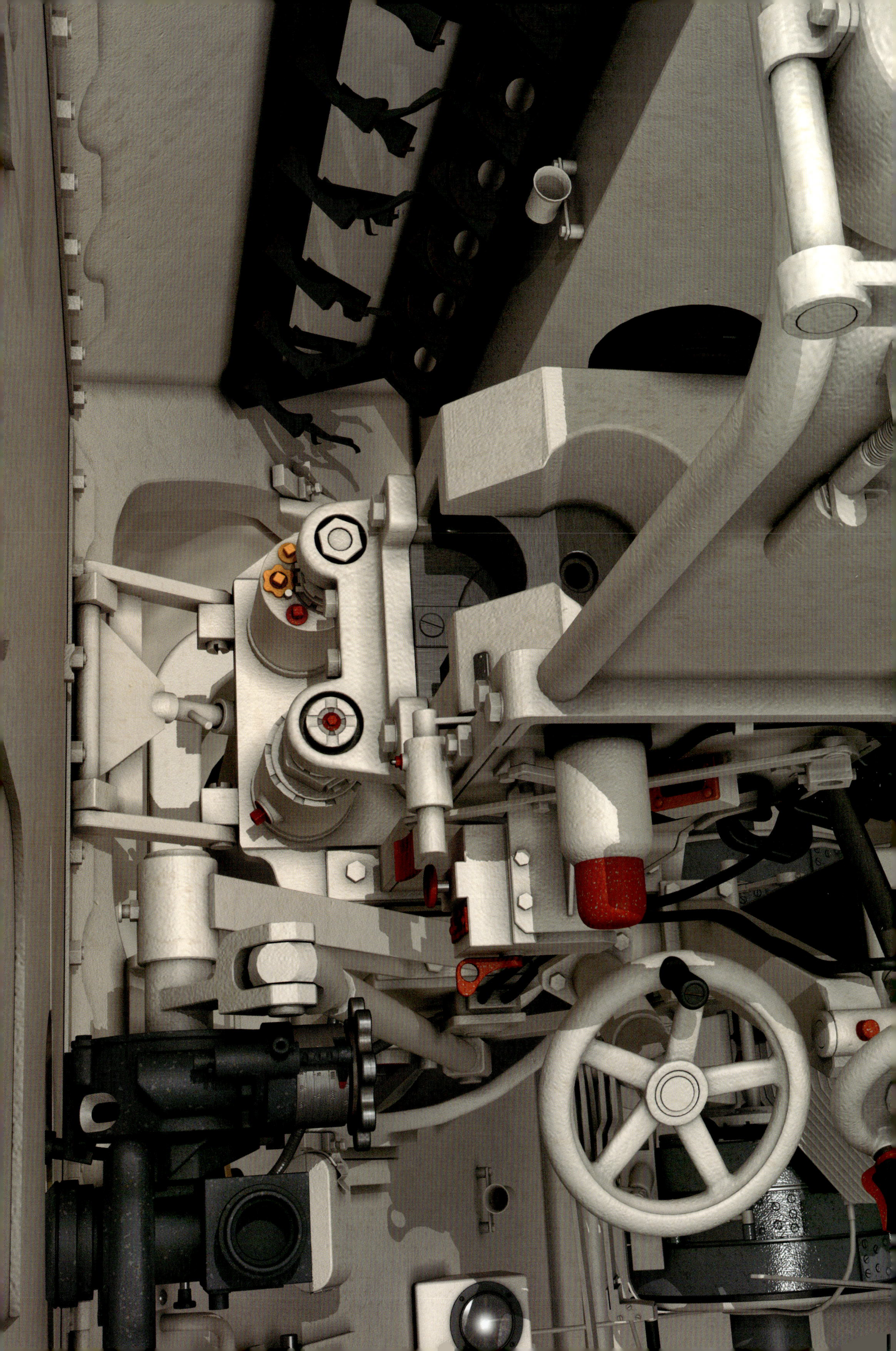

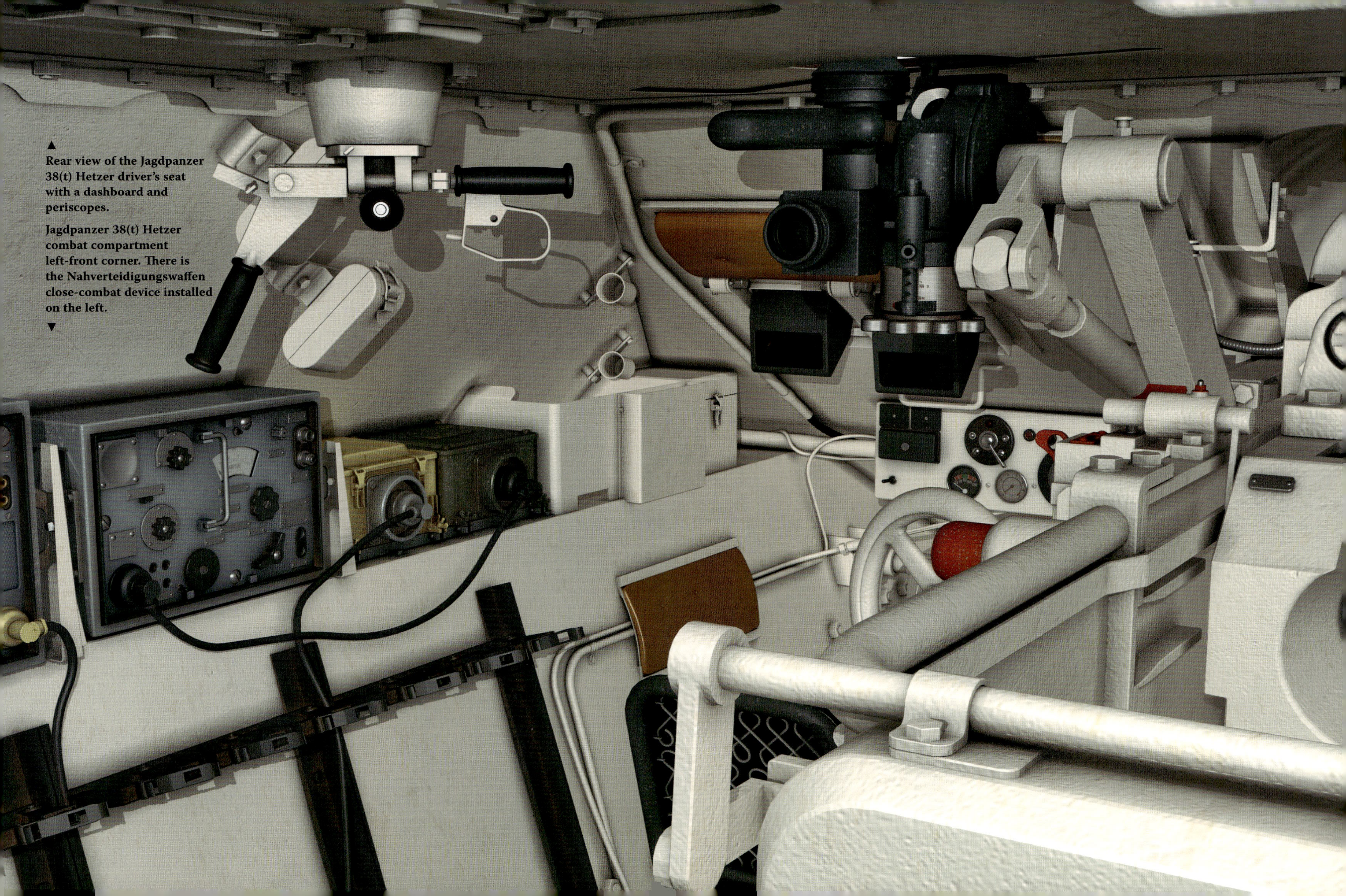

▲ Rear view of the Jagdpanzer 38(t) Hetzer driver's seat with a dashboard and periscopes.

Jagdpanzer 38(t) Hetzer combat compartment left-front corner. There is the Nahverteidigungswaffen close-combat device installed on the left. ▼

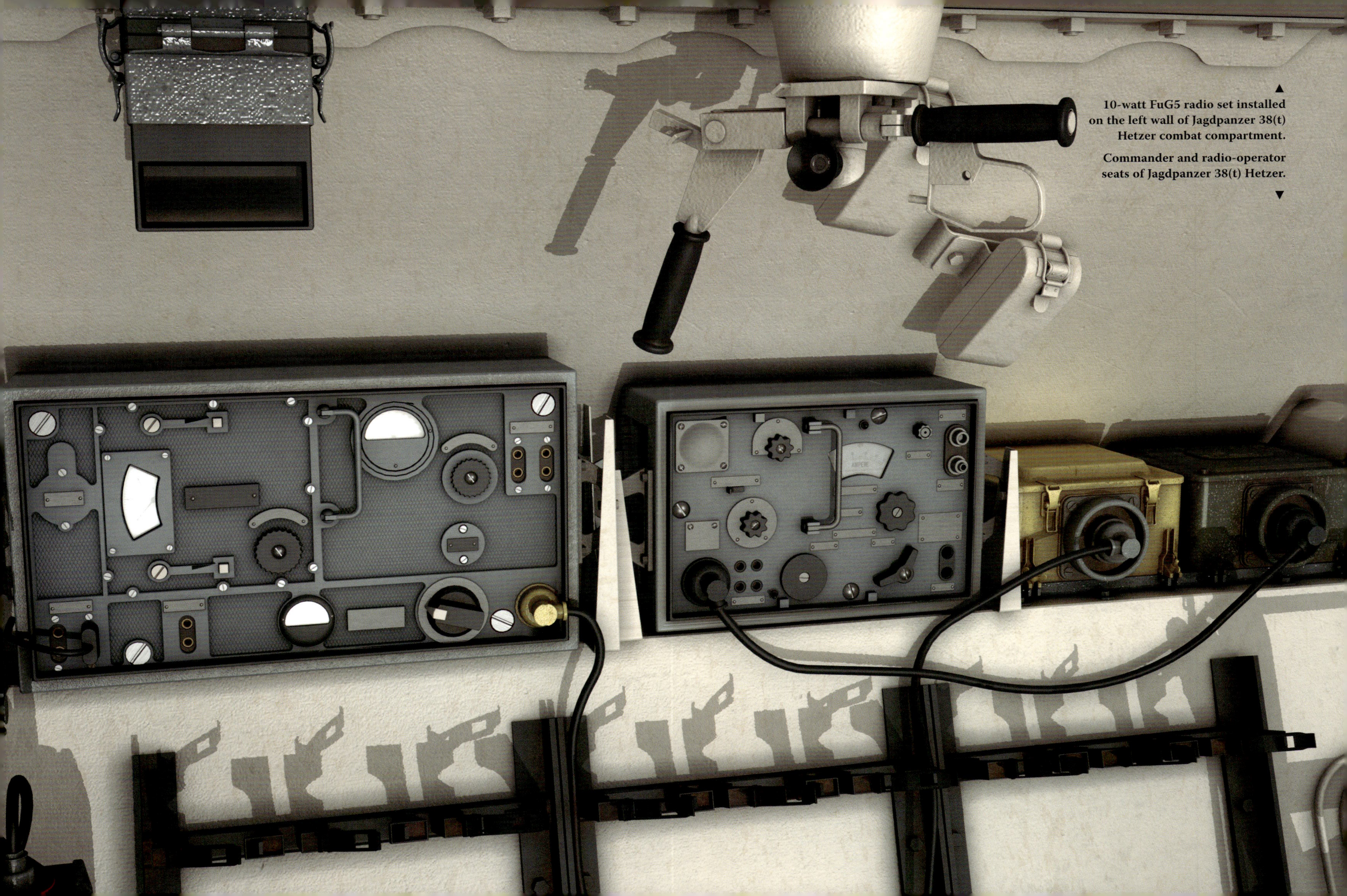

▲ 10-watt FuG5 radio set installed on the left wall of Jagdpanzer 38(t) Hetzer combat compartment.

Commander and radio-operator seats of Jagdpanzer 38(t) Hetzer. ▼

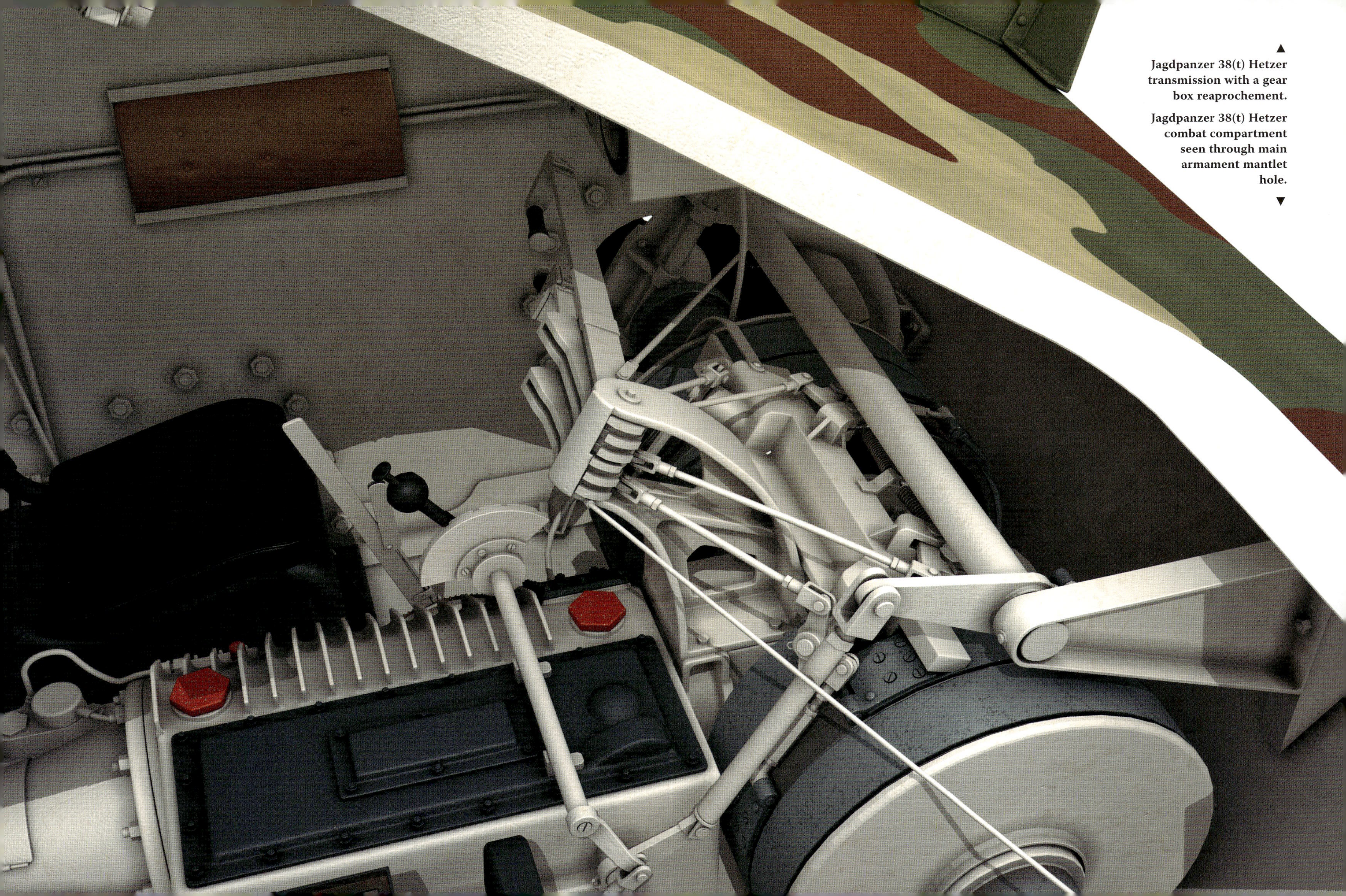

▲ Jagdpanzer 38(t) Hetzer transmission with a gear box reaprochement.

Jagdpanzer 38(t) Hetzer combat compartment seen through main armament mantlet hole. ▼

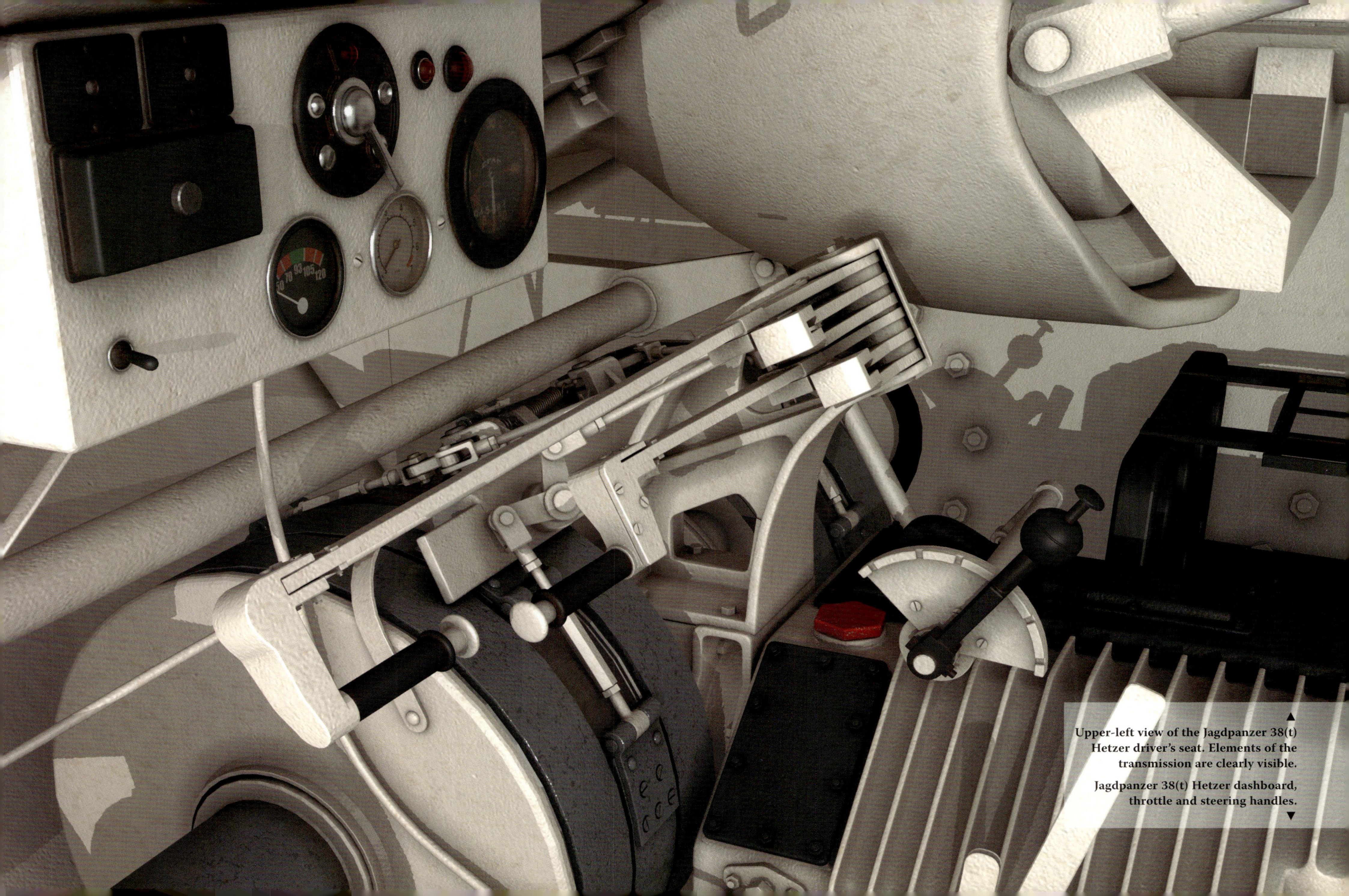


▲ Upper-left view of the Jagdpanzer 38(t) Hetzer driver's seat. Elements of the transmission are clearly visible.

Jagdpanzer 38(t) Hetzer dashboard, throttle and steering handles. ▼

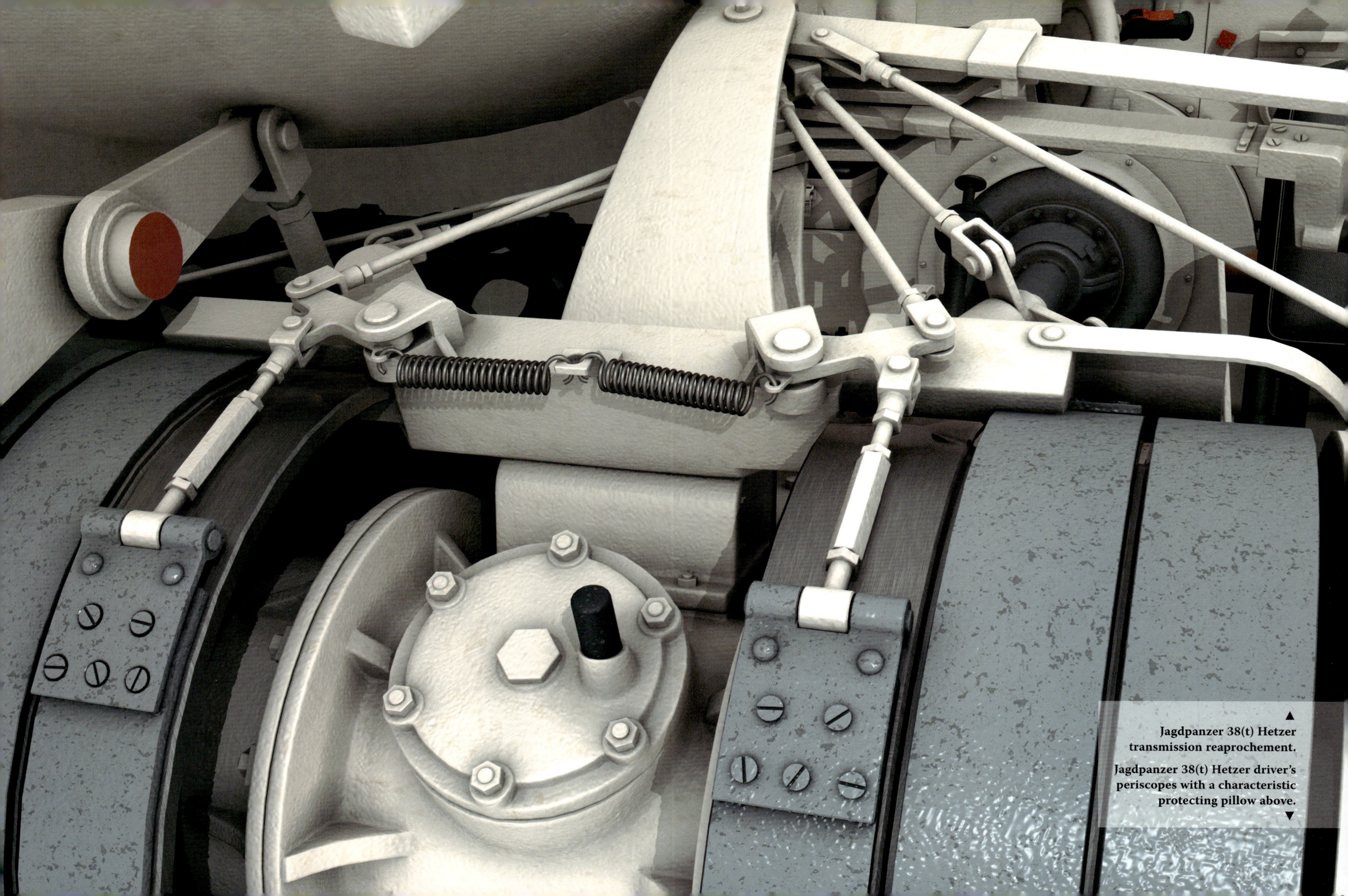

▲ Jagdpanzer 38(t) Hetzer transmission reaprochement.

Jagdpanzer 38(t) Hetzer driver's periscopes with a characteristic protecting pillow above. ▼

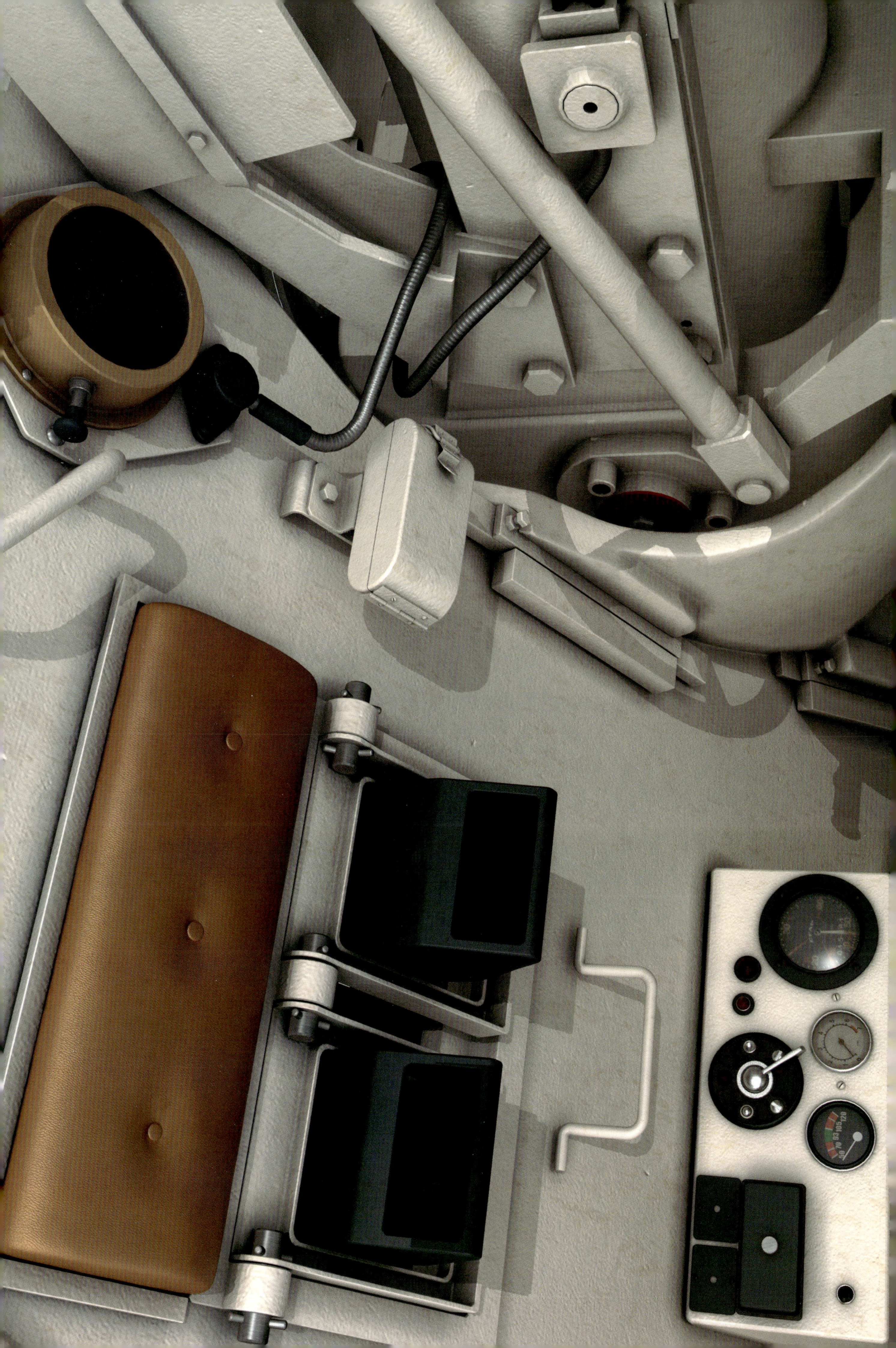

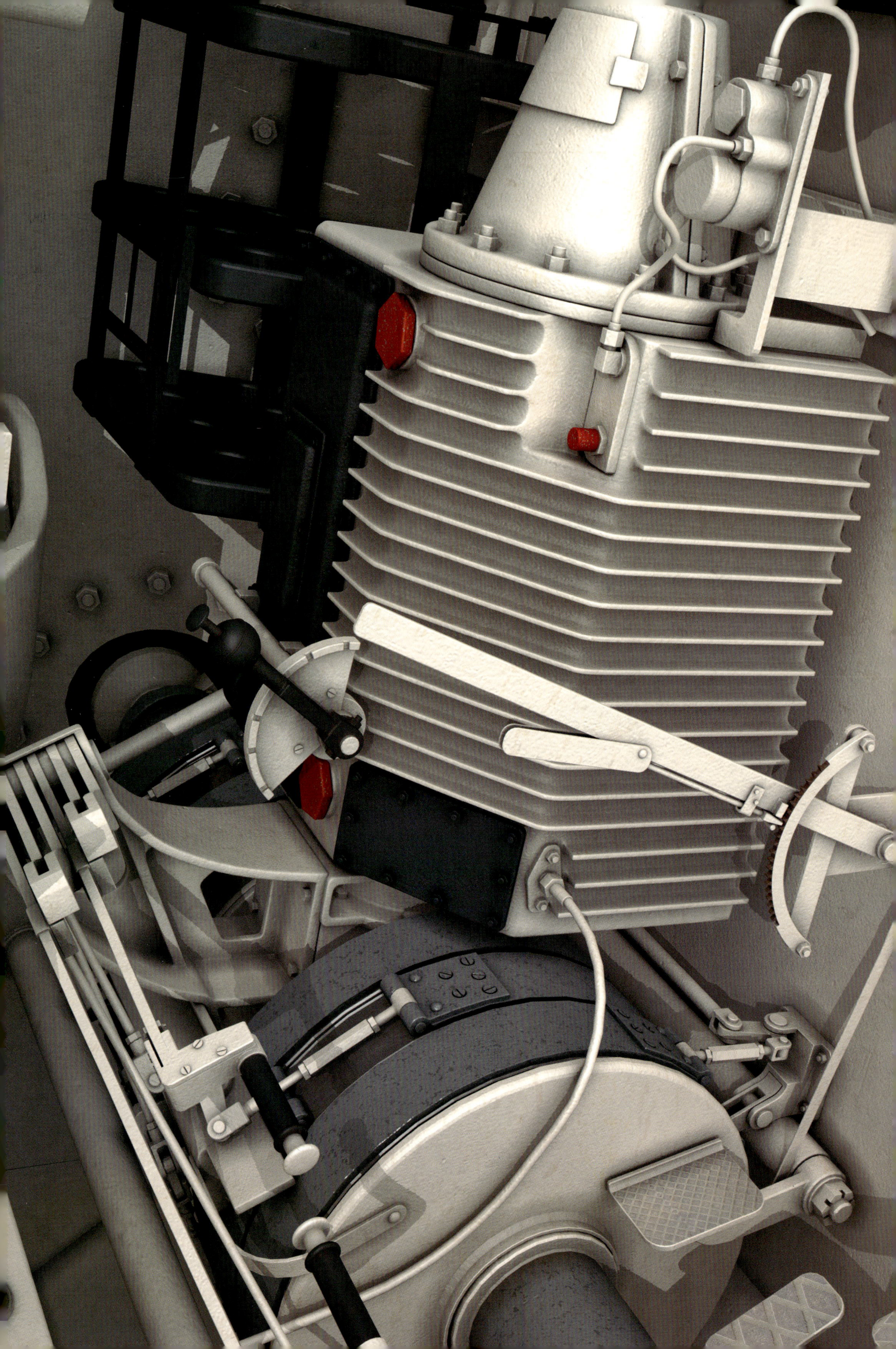

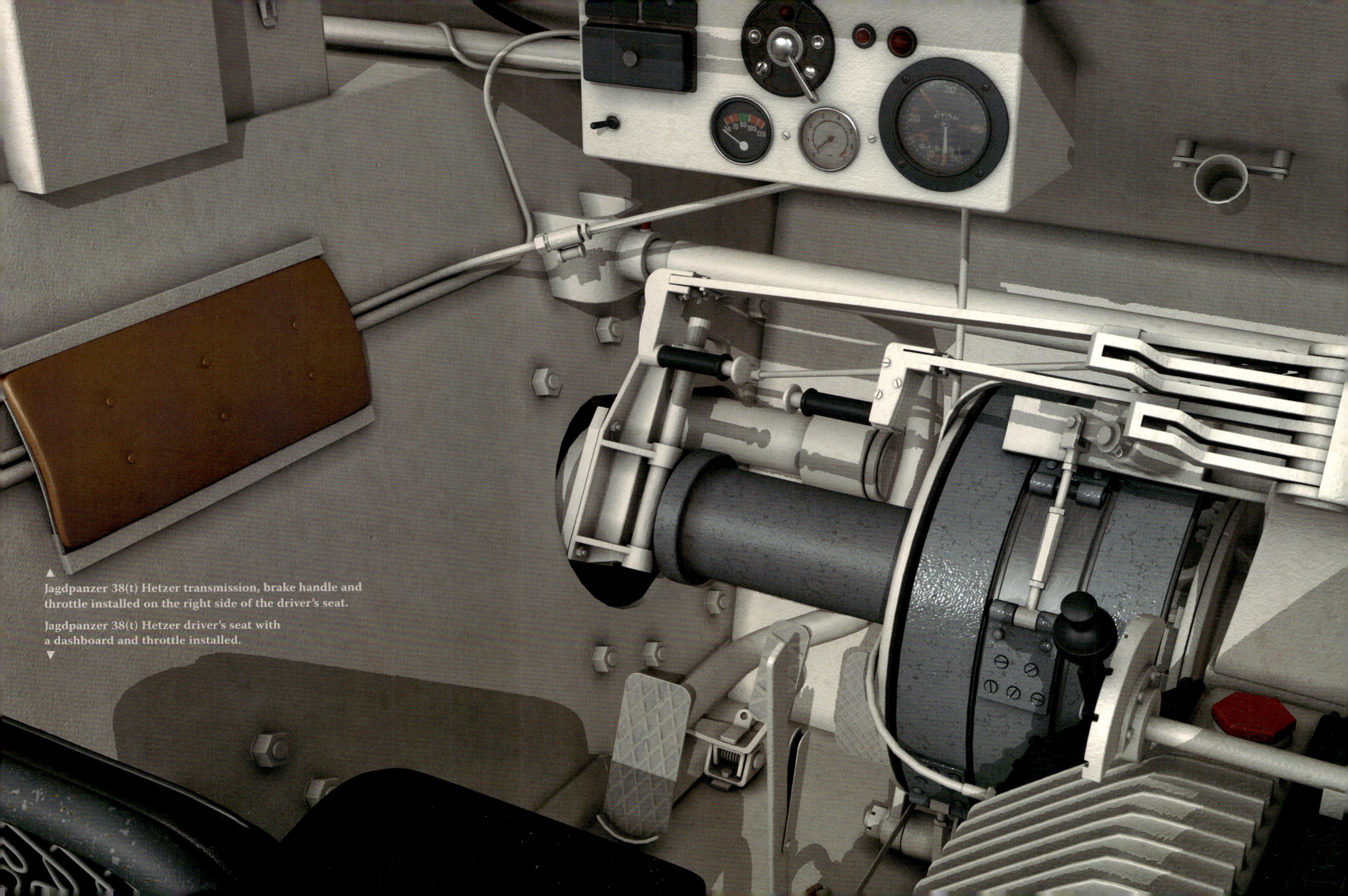

▲ Jagdpanzer 38(t) Hetzer transmission, brake handle and throttle installed on the right side of the driver's seat.

Jagdpanzer 38(t) Hetzer driver's seat with a dashboard and throttle installed. ▼

▲ Part of the G-13 main armament as well as driver's seat seen from behind.

FuG5 radio set in all its glory. There are rifle-butt mountings installed on the wall above the device. ▼

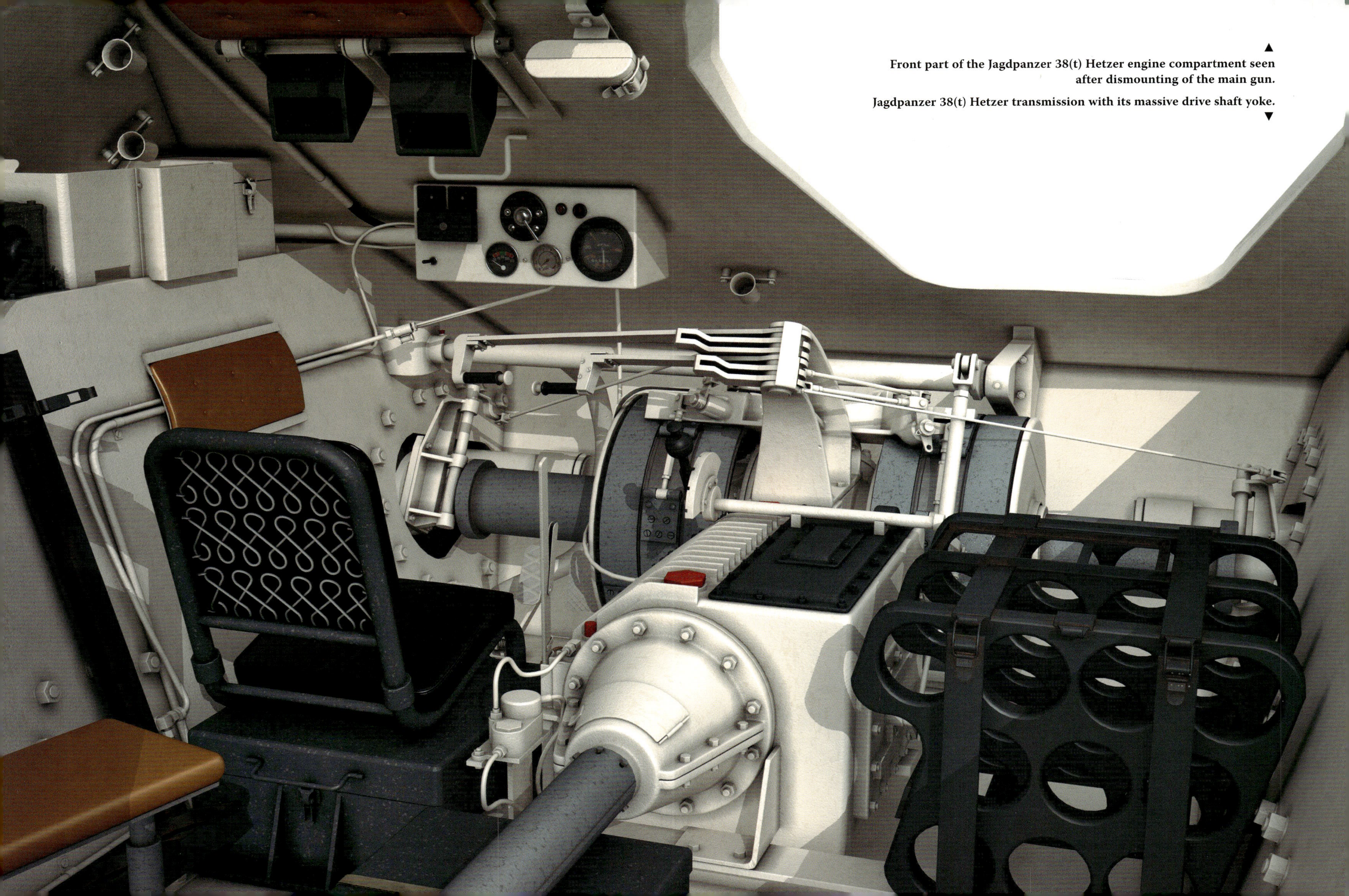

▲ Front part of the Jagdpanzer 38(t) Hetzer engine compartment seen after dismounting of the main gun.

Jagdpanzer 38(t) Hetzer transmission with its massive drive shaft yoke. ▼